The Pennsylvania Horticultural Society presents

The PHS City Parks Handbook

Writers
Jane Carroll, Daniel Moise, Joan Reilly

Contributors
Maitreyi Roy, PHS Parks Team,
PHS Public Landscapes Design & Management Team, Paul Bonfanti

DVD production
Margaret Funderburg

Graphic Design
Eliza Leydon

The Pennsylvania Horticultural Society
100 N. 20th Street
Philadelphia, PA 19103
215-988-8800
fax: 215-988-8810
www.pennsylvaniahorticulturalsociety.org

President: Jane G. Pepper
Executive Vice President: J. Blaine Bonham, Jr.
Vice President, Programs: Maitreyi Roy
Philadelphia Green Senior Director: Joan Reilly
Publications Director: Pete Prown

Acknowledgments

THIS PROJECT WAS FINANCED (IN PART) BY A GRANT FROM THE COMMONWEALTH
OF PENNSYLVANIA, DEPARTMENT OF COMMUNITY AND ECONOMIC DEVELOPMENT

PHS would like to thank:

The network of park friends groups throughout Philadelphia

Philadelphia Department of Recreation

The Fairmount Park Commission

Philadelphia Department of Public Property

Philadelphia Parks Alliance

The City Parks Alliance

Betsie Blodgett

Virginia Claire McGuire

PHS is grateful to the following funders of the Philadelphia Green Parks Revitalization Project:

Alliance for Community Trees

Anonymous

Bank of America Foundation

Boeing Company, Defense & Space Group

Citizens Bank Foundation

City of Philadelphia, Office of Housing and Community Development

ERM Group Foundation

Samuel S. Fels Fund

Fox & Roach Charities

Walter J. Miller Trust

PA Department of Community and Economic Development

The Philadelphia Committee of the Garden Club of America

William Penn Foundation

© 2009 The Pennsylvania Horticultural Society

ISBN Number 978-0-615-26081-5

Record Number 93086

Table of Contents

Chapter 1: Introduction

INTRODUCTION

The Pennsylvania Horticultural Society is pleased to present the *PHS City Parks Handbook* as a resource for those who care about creating, reclaiming, and maintaining urban parks. In many cities, park management is no longer the sole province of government, and committed citizens are increasingly becoming involved in park stewardship. At the same time, cities across America are beginning to recognize that investments in parks and other green spaces pay big economic dividends and are viewing them as an essential component of urban revitalization. This manual shows how volunteers, community organizations, and government—working together in partnership—can create thriving green spaces that not only provide fresh air and beauty, but also help build stronger communities and more livable cities.

The Value of Urban Parks

Parks provide significant *aesthetic*, *economic*, *environmental*, and *social* benefits to cities. They add beauty to the urban scene, provide relief from the noise and grit of city life, and reflect the history and culture of their neighborhoods. They are play spaces for children and give adults a place to gather with neighbors. Parks are a source of community pride and offer fresh air and breathing room for all.

Even the smallest park can have a positive impact on the quality of life for residents. Parks promote social interaction and serve as communal "front yards." Studies show that proximity to parks improves health by offering opportunities for recreation and exercise—free of charge. Attractive, well-used parks also help reduce crime by signaling a safe, stable neighborhood and fostering an environment where residents are deeply invested in their community. What's more, parks reduce vandalism by youth. In a report published by the Trust for Public Land, Paul M. Sherer writes, "Recreational facilities keep at-risk youth off the streets, give them a safe environment to interact with their peers, and fill up time within which they could otherwise get into trouble."

Well-kept parks and public green spaces boost urban economies. They create a positive impression for visitors and make cities more appealing to tourists. Good parks also help cities attract and retain residents along with the businesses that employ them. Research shows that "knowledge workers" prefer to live in places with a wealth of outdoor recreational opportunities, and many newer companies look for those amenities when choosing a location.

Moreover, parks increase the real-estate value of nearby properties, thereby generating additional tax revenue for the entire city. This effect has been documented since the nineteenth century, when property values rose dramatically in New York City after the creation of Central Park.

In *Urban Parks and Open Space*, Alexander Garvin writes, "These park-generated revenues allowed the city to pay for municipal services that it could not otherwise have afforded and provided the stimulus for city officials to acquire the 26,369 acres of land that currently constitute New York City's extraordinary park system."

Parks are part of the "green infrastructure" that improves the local environment of cities in several ways. Green open spaces prevent flooding by absorbing rainwater and improve water quality by filtering out impurities. Trees in parks clean the air by absorbing pollutants and releasing oxygen, reducing costs associated with health care and pollution remediation. By moderating summer temperatures, trees also keep buildings cooler; reduce the need for air-conditioning; and lessen the "heat island" effect of large metropolitan areas, in which temperatures in and around large cities can be significantly higher than in outlying areas. Trees and other plants also create habitat for birds and insects, which are an important part of the ecosystem.

For all these reasons, great parks have a vital role to play in the "green revolution" that promises to transform America's cities and towns. Providing a high quality of life is a top priority for twenty-first-century American cities competing for jobs and residents, and greener cities are coming out ahead.

Transforming Parks

PHS's Philadelphia Green program launched the Parks Revitalization Project in 1993 through a grant from the Philadelphia-based William Penn Foundation. From the outset, the project was conceived as a partnership between Philadelphia Green, city government, and citizen volunteers.

Envisioned by its founder, William Penn, as a "Green Countrie Towne," Philadelphia has one of the largest urban park systems in the United States, including large watershed parks and hundreds of neighborhood parks. But by the early 1990s, Philadelphia, like many other post-industrial cities, suffered from shrinking municipal budgets and declining federal support. Funding for parks was cut, and many parks in the city showed serious signs of neglect; quite a few had become hotspots of drug and gang activity. In short, parks that once served as centers of community life had become dangerous eyesores.

Beginning with just three parks—Vernon Park in Germantown, Norris Square Park in eastern North Philadelphia, and Wharton Square Park in South Philadelphia—Philadelphia Green organized neighborhood volunteers into independent "friends" groups that serve as park stewards. At the same time, it offered training and technical support to staff of the city's Department of Recreation, which oversees many neighborhood parks. Philadelphia Green served as the catalyst for a working partnership that has leveraged increased support for neighborhood parks throughout the city.

The PHS parks project now encompasses approximately 100 parks. The Fairmount Park system, with governance of 9,200 acres of city parkland, has joined the partnership, contributing the experience it has gained through working with its own friends groups since the 1980s. Park groups organize regular workdays, raise funds, recruit volunteers, and reach out to neighborhood partners. Twice each year the partnership hosts major citywide cleanups that involve thousands of volunteers. A steering committee consisting of park leaders, PHS staff, the Philadelphia Parks Alliance (the city's leading park advocacy organization), and representatives of Fairmount Park and the Department of Recreation meets five times yearly to facilitate communication and planning.

The Philadelphia Green Parks Revitalization Project is a dynamic, enduring partnership that has transformed parks throughout the city. Neighborhood parks are buzzing with activity, hosting celebrations, volunteer workdays, concerts, and farmers markets. Residents have been empowered to reclaim their parks and their communities.

How to Use this Manual

This manual offers information and resources to help volunteers develop the organizational skills, knowledge, and partnerships necessary to reclaim their parks. Topics range from creating the organizational framework for your group to raising funds to running a workday and beyond. Although the advice contained in this book draws on the experiences of the PHS Philadelphia Green program, it is our hope that these lessons will be useful to cities and towns across the nation.

The accompanying DVD contains inspiring stories that will help motivate your group. On it you will find insightful interviews with PHS staff members, city government employees, and park activists that shed light on the process of reclaiming a park and show the dramatic transformations that can happen when people work together. The DVD also contains instructions on tree planting, as well as a story about involving youth in park activities.

The team at Philadelphia Green hopes this manual will help guide you through this rewarding process. As you proceed, please keep the manual on hand and refer to it as questions arise. Additional information can be found at the PHS website, *www.pennsylvaniahorticulturalsociety.org* or by contacting the PHS parks staff at 215-988-8800.

Even the smallest park can have a positive impact on the quality of life.

About the Pennsylvania Horticultural Society

The Pennsylvania Horticultural Society (PHS) is a nonprofit membership organization founded in 1827. PHS produces the **Philadelphia Flower Show®**, the world's largest indoor flower show, and offers events, workshops, activities, and publications for novice gardeners, experienced horticulturists, and plant lovers of all ages.

For more than 30 years, PHS's **Philadelphia Green®** program has been forging successful partnerships and empowering communities to transform key landscapes, raise awareness of greening issues, and support best practices in open-space management. The nation's most comprehensive greening program, Philadelphia Green works closely with community residents to improve parks and commercial corridors, start community gardens, plant trees, and clean and green vacant land—breathing new life into neighborhoods that have suffered from years of disinvestment. Philadelphia Green restores and manages high-profile civic landscapes, playing a pivotal role in Philadelphia's renaissance as a vibrant destination city.

Philadelphia Green promotes investment in the city's landscape infrastructure as a critical part of long-term community revitalization efforts, using horticulture as a tool to build community and improve the quality of life. With Philadelphia Green's support, community gardeners and inmates of the Philadelphia Prison System cultivate and donate organically grown produce for low-income families. In collaboration with the Philadelphia Water Department, Philadelphia Green works to develop innovative landscape designs and create green corridors to help manage stormwater. Philadelphia Green sets a standard of excellence for open space improvement and promotes innovative best practices and policies for creating a green, sustainable city.

In recent years, PHS has expanded the reach of its greening initiatives **beyond Philadelphia's borders**. PHS is a lead partner in TreeVitalize, a program of the Pennsylvania Department of Conservation and Natural Resources that seeks to restore the depleted tree canopy in metropolitan areas. PHS also partners with the Pennsylvania Downtown Center and with Keep Pennsylvania Beautiful, participating in KPB's summer internship program for college students and jointly running a statewide open-space recognition program called the Community Greening Award. PHS's goal is to reach out and serve as a resource for cities throughout the nation that use greening as a tool for revitalization.

PHS **education** programs include hundreds of engaging programs year-round for gardeners, children, teachers, and community leaders. Educational endeavors about gardening, horticulture, and improving public spaces are intrinsic to the PHS mission and enrich the lives of people throughout the region. The PHS **McLean Library** holds 15,000 volumes on gardening, botany, and urban greening and includes historical and rare books and catalogs from the past six centuries. The Library's "Ask a Gardener" phone and email service answers gardening questions from across the country. The **Gold Medal Plant Award program** selects and promotes reliable woody plants for gardeners in the Mid-Atlantic region.

Visitors at the Philadelphia Flower Show

A volunteer planting near City Hall

A PHS partnership with government agencies and other nonprofits

A free gardening workshop for city residents

Chapter 2: Taking the First Steps

Forming your Friends Group

If you're reading this, it's clear you're determined to make your local park the best that it can be. Step one toward achieving this goal is forming a "friends of the park" group. This is a journey that requires commitment, but it is rewarding and great fun, too.

All you need to form a friends group is people. It's that simple. Whether your group consists of four people or 40 is entirely up to you—there is no magic number. However, the larger the group, the more organized you need to be.

Attract potential group members by running an advertisement in the local papers, hanging flyers in the park, or talking to neighbors. Let people know from the start what kind of commitment they'd be making. Tell those who would like to help, but can't fully commit, that you'll need volunteers in the future. Never burn a bridge.

A park group will function best with a shared vision that includes a stated purpose, priorities, and plan of action.

Getting Started

When the time comes for the first meeting—which can be held in a living room as easily as a public library or recreation center—give all those who attend the opportunity to say their reasons for attending and their concerns for the park. Initiate a dialog that gets people talking about the role of the friends group and the sort of projects it should tackle. Also, reserve time to brainstorm a group name. Choose a meeting moderator whose job is to keep people focused and make sure all opinions are welcomed and encouraged.

At this first meeting and throughout the weeks ahead, the group should work toward conceiving a "shared vision." Individual input is essential, and, at the same time, everyone needs to be on the same page in order to move forward. Determine the group's purpose, its hopes for the park, and how it will accomplish its goals. If you like, articulate your intentions by developing a mission statement. Use it as a way of communicating your ideas with potential partners.

For large groups, you may want to draft formal policies or bylaws regarding certain matters, like the way money is spent or the system for selecting leaders. These should not be murky matters; avoid headaches by establishing a clear system from the beginning.

The decision-making process can make or break a park group, so resolve this matter early on. There are many ways for a group to make decisions (see "How to Reach a Group Decision" on page 15). A group may also decide to use different decision-making styles depending on the issue. Always be clear who gets to make decisions and by what method.

Discuss matters that will help establish your group's working policies. For instance, decide whether to institute annual membership fees. Would dues be effective? If so, how would those funds be spent (e.g., refreshments, advertisements, tools and supplies)? Remember, membership dues may deter some people, but the plus side is that others will be more inclined to remain active if they are financially invested.

Consider ways to make your park and group more visible to the larger community. Group T-shirts can help solidify your group's presence and commitment. Perhaps a local business can be persuaded to cover the printing costs if allowed to advertise on the back. Ultimately, everyone in the neighborhood will know that the people in the certain-colored shirts are dedicated park stewards. It also quickly informs new residents of your presence.

Remember that people are coming together because they care about the park. While you want to create a plan of action, don't get bogged down in too much talk and planning at the beginning. Organize workdays, events, and activities that allow people to do what they care about most: spend time in the park. Park revitalization is a long journey, and early-action projects help build momentum.

Meetings provide the opportunity to get organized, share information, plan, solve problems, evaluate, and celebrate your group's work. Regularly scheduled meetings keep the lines of communication open and help keep the group on task, while special meetings may be necessary when issues arise that need focused attention. That said, never have a meeting just to meet. If you have nothing to discuss, don't hesitate to cancel a meeting. Respect people's time and strive to conduct meetings that are focused and productive.

When organizing a meeting, ask yourself:

- *What is the purpose of the meeting?*
- *What will people know, feel, and do as a result of attending the meeting?*

Assign Roles
Decide who will manage or facilitate the meeting and who will introduce which topics. Assign someone to take notes.

Set the Agenda
Once you are clear on the purpose of the meeting, draw up an agenda. Decide who should attend and what will be discussed. Think carefully about what you need to cover and the amount of time you have to cover it. Do not try to do too much. Allow time at the end of the meeting for review.

Decision-Making
Decision-making is an area where many meetings break down. Be sure participants understand their role in the process. One size doesn't fit all; it's important to be clear about how the decision will be made prior to calling for a vote.

What if the group is not ready to make a decision? Determine what people need in order to take a position. Do they simply need more time to consider the issues? Do they need more information? Based on these needs, identify the next steps with a division of labor and a time frame.

Who will Do What by When?
It's important to conclude a meeting with a good sense of the "next steps" or a to-do list. List upcoming initiatives and clarify the

Park groups discuss a shared vision for their park.

task, division of labor, and time frame necessary to keep the work moving forward.

Dealing with Conflict
Each member of the group comes with a distinct set of experiences and viewpoints. Conflicts are inevitable and present a challenge for many groups. If handled poorly, conflicts can tear a group apart, so the tendency is to avoid them. Resolving conflicts in a constructive way requires skill, patience, and courage. The following tips will help you navigate conflicts, but they are useful skills for any meeting facilitator:

Active Listening
Listen carefully with an open mind to what people are saying. Don't finish other people's sentences or prepare a defense while someone else is speaking. Remember, listening is an active, not passive, pursuit.

Paraphrase
Repeat what you are hearing, without judgment, and check for accuracy. "So what I'm hearing is …. Is that what you mean?"

Summarize
Summarize the different points of view.

Analyze
Have the group think about the pros and cons of each position.

Resolve or Advance
Find out if the group is ready to make a decision or come to an agreement about how to proceed. If they are not, ask what they need to move forward, such as more time to think about it, more time to discuss the issue, or a third party to help mediate.

How to Reach a Group Decision

- **Consensus**: An opinion or position agreed to by the group as a whole
- **Simple Majority**: A number of voters constituting more than half the total
- **Two-thirds Majority**: The number of votes for a proposition equaling or exceeding twice the number of votes against it
- **Plurality**: The largest voting bloc, even if it falls short of a majority of the group
- **Range Voting**: Participants rank or score the available options using a point system

Planning for a better park

The Meeting Menu

A well-thought-out agenda is like a delicious meal, served with great care and intention. Consider running a meeting that features multiple courses, and decide who you want around the table to ensure a good outcome.

The first course is the appetizer. It's a chance to whet the appetite—to welcome people, share the purpose of the meeting, and set the context.

The second and third courses are the substance of the meeting. Serve enough, but not too much. When you try to address a large number of important topics, you can leave people with too much to digest.

Enjoy dessert at the end of the meal. The close of the meeting should be memorable and positive. This is when you review decisions and next steps. It's also the opportunity to thank people for their efforts and reflect on what was accomplished. End at the promised time or earlier. Keep the "dessert" sweet and leave the "guests" hungry for more.

Communicate with your Park Group Online

Thanks to the Internet, it's easier than ever to communicate with your park group. Let's look at a few ways you can use your mouse to stay in touch:

Email

Aside from direct, person-to-person email messages, the simplest way to communicate online is by creating a group (or distribution list) in your email program. Most programs allow the user to create a group by adding a number of email addresses and then saving them under one name (such as "My Park Group"). Then, whenever you type "My Park Group" into the address line, everyone on your distribution list will receive that email.

Blogging

A blog is a web page that allows people to post messages and photographs, and others to read them and sometimes even respond. On many sites, the creator of the blog can designate who is allowed to write and read messages. This can be perfect for a park group, since someone can post dates and times for a workday, or even post photos of a recent event.

WEB SOURCES:
blogspot.com and *livejournal.com*

Groups

Another popular choice for communication is an electronic mailing list or web forum. For example, a Yahoo or Google group is a web-oriented group formed around a single subject, from very broad topics (such as "All about Gardening") to a very specific topic (such as one about your local park group).

After it's launched, the group "moderator" can decide who he or she wants to let join. All members of your group can write messages and respond to messages by others.

WEB SOURCES:
yahoogroups.com and
groups.google.com

Web Calendars

This is a service (often free) that allows groups to share an online calendar. Members of these groups can post events and receive reminders of upcoming events.

WEB SOURCES:
google.com/calendar and
calendar.yahoo.com

Building a Website

If you have the time and resources, some park groups may choose to create their own website with their own name in the address (such as *YourParkGroup.org*). A website can be very simple—just a few pages with basic information, work dates, and a photo or two.

Self-Built Sites

Many popular Internet providers give their members free web-building software, as well as a small amount of server space to host their new website for free (this is because websites require physical hard-drive space to exist). Check with your provider for more information on these self-built and often free sites.

WEB SOURCES:
igoogle.com, aol.com,
earthlink.com, and
joomla.org

Using a Web Developer… or a Friend!

If you have the financial resources, a park group could hire a web developer to build a site for your park group. The developer will meet with you to discuss functions you need your site to fulfill and then help you to design the required pages. Part of the project will also include agreeing on a price for their services and a timetable for completion. You should also talk about long-term hosting of the site, as well as who will update information on the site.

WEB SOURCES:
web-development.com and
freelancedesigners.com

Another alternative is to ask a tech-savvy friend to build your site for free or at a discount. Sometimes this is the easiest and most affordable way to build a dedicated website. Just be clear on the roles and expectations; talk about what you expect from the site and when you'll need it (nothing slows down a project more than unclear roles). And, as with all volunteers, remember to say "Thank you!"

Please note that while the Internet is a tremendous resource, there are likely some people involved with the park who do not use computers regularly. Ensure that these people are not excluded from park happenings and that there are alternative means of disseminating information.

Don't trick yourself into thinking you can do this alone; even history's greatest leaders benefited from the support of others. And remember, every person has certain skills, resources, or connections that can further your work.

A Philadelphia Green Story
One Person Can Make a Difference

A journey into West Philadelphia reveals a true urban oasis. Malcolm X Memorial Park spans an entire city block, and these days it's filled with activity. This is a stark contrast to what the space once was. Not that long ago, the park was unused and unsafe. Budget cuts prohibited legitimate attempts to restore it, and the crumbling walkways, neglected trees, and trashy interior made the park a liability to the neighborhood. Fortunately, there were certain individuals who could look past the blight and see the park's potential as a community gathering place.

Gregorio "Greg" Pac Cojulun Jr. is one of the people who helped guide the park back to its current vibrancy. Since retiring in the late 1980s, he's been anything but idle. For more than a decade, he has served as president of the Friends of Malcolm X Memorial Park. "Greg's always meeting and greeting people in the park," observes Philadelphia Green's C. R. Robinson, adding that people call him "the mayor" or "the ambassador" of the park.

To get the friends group off the ground, Greg forged partnerships with the Philadelphia Department of Recreation and Philadelphia Green, a collaboration he describes as "tremendous." He specifically credits Philadelphia Green for passing on the know-how and resources for things like garden supplies, flowers, seeds, planters, and an inventory of the park's tree population.

Others have contributed to the park's resurgence as well. Children's Hospital of Philadelphia leads safety workshops for the neighborhood kids and funded the park's play equipment. Teachers from local schools have organized classes to take part in an after-school "Park Patrol" to help keep the park clean. "And our city councilwoman, Jannie Blackwell, has been a big help as well," adds Greg.

He also gives ample credit to the area police. Greg worked hard to get increased patrols of the park and to have police in attendance at events and celebrations. By doing so, the community understood the park was safe to visit.

Two interconnected lessons can be learned from Greg's success. The first is that a strong-willed, committed park leader is capable of tremendous things. The second lesson is that good leaders link with the community and develop strong partnerships that maximize the effects of his or her efforts.

Malcolm X Memorial Park keeps a busy schedule of events. The park's friends group is led by
Gregorio Pac Cojulun Jr. (inset).

Conducting a Park Inventory

Once your group is established, one of the first items on the agenda should be creating a park inventory. A park inventory is a detailed picture of your park as it is now. Some park inventories are based on written checklists, others on maps. It should be easy to read and paint a complete picture of the park's physical features and condition. An inventory will help you plan and prioritize your group's goals. It is a precursor to a more comprehensive master plan (see Chapter 4). The inventory document should address the following topics:

- **What the park currently offers**
- **How it serves the community**
- **What would make it even better**

1. The first step is to walk through the park and document what you see. Record landscape elements, such as trees, shrubs, plantings, and lawns. How many benches are there? What is the lighting situation? Are there buildings, fountains, or playgrounds on the premises? For a sample checklist, see page 22.

2. Alternatively, use a map to collect this information or to accompany the checklist. Find out if the city or landowner has a map you can use for reference. If not, create your own informal map, or use Google Earth (download for free at *www.googleearth.com*). Indicate the location of park features on the map.

3. As you survey the park's offerings, be sure to note their condition. Are the water fountains flowing smoothly or are they rundown and rusty? Do the trees require pruning? Take note of any problems needing immediate attention.

4. Next, identify the park's stakeholders. Find out who uses the park, for what purposes, and when. At the same time, find out if some segment of the neighborhood is not using the park and why. For example, is the playground in such bad condition that children avoid it? Interview people who use the park regularly. You may have certain ideas for the park's future, but are they in sync with those of your neighbors? Ask them what they like about the park and what suggestions they have to improve it.

5. The final step is compiling the above information in an organized way. Assign someone to put the findings on the page (or on a computer). Give everyone a chance to review the first draft to make sure it's complete.

Working as a group, begin to determine what you'd like to accomplish in the weeks, months, and years ahead. Compile a list of possible enhancements. Each park landscape is different. The park's size, location, and usage patterns will all come into play as you develop a vision for your park. If you consider your park to be a seven now, what would make it a 10? Are planting beds full of weeds? Are there too few trashcans? Make a list of what needs addressing and the steps toward the desired end result.

The inventory is a great tool for staying organized and informing others about your park. The inventory should also make clear what projects are of main concern, and therefore influence future workdays and fundraisers.

Through the years, make updates to the inventory, especially after the completion of major projects. This should be a living document; don't let it become dated and useless. Clearly charting your progress builds a sense of accomplishment and lets you see how far your park has come.

A group conducts a park inventory.

Park Inventory Sample

Below is a sample park inventory; use it as a template when forming your own. Each park is different, so be sure to add anything specific to your park that isn't found here. When improvements are made, be sure to reflect that in the inventory. If updated regularly, a spreadsheet like this can keep your group organized and focused.

GREENFIELD PARK INVENTORY - Updated 10/05/2008

Item	Description	Quantity	Poor	Adequate	Good	Very Good	Excellent	Notes
HARDSCAPE								
Benches	wooden, 8 years old	9			X			Top Priority: Getting new trash cans (current ones are in poor shape) and installing recycling bins alongside. The mural is fading, but okay for the time being.
Playground Equipment	just installed						X	
Slides	just installed						X	
Swings	just installed	4					X	
Monkey Bars	N/A							
Fences	brand new							
Retaining Walls								
Planters	cement urns by garden	2				X		
Park Art	lion sculpture, mural	2			X			
Signs and Banners								
Entrance	"Welcome" sign	1				X		
Perimeter	N/A							
Rules/Regulations	by restrooms	2			X			
Trash Cans	metal, no lids	10		X				
Recycling Cans	N/A							
Flag Poles	N/A							
Dog-Related Items								
Litter Bag Dispenser	just installed	2					X	
Dog Run	just installed	1					X	
Other								
SOFTSCAPE								
Trees	mostly oak/maple/pine	28			X			West lawn needs grass seed, need to remove dying oak tree by the fountain.
Bushes / Shrubs	rhododendrons	12				X		
Flower Beds	N/A							
Turf / Grass					X			
Playing Fields	baseball, volleyball	2				X		
BUILDINGS								
Exterior	rec. center					X		Mostly fine. Install A/C before next summer?
Interior						X		
Roof	repaired 05/2004						X	
Doorways		3				X		
Windows		7		X				
Facilities								
Gazebo	N/A							
Storage Shed	attached to restrooms				X			
WALKWAYS								
Perimeter						X		The southside parking lot needs to be repaved. Need to pull weeds by the walkways.
Interior						X		
Trails	N/A							
Parking Areas		2	X		X			
ELECTRIC								
Perimeter	installed 07/1999	8				X		Posts in fine condition. Add more lighting to parking lot for safety?
Interior	installed 07/1999	6				X		
Light Post Condition						X		
WATER								
Water Outlets/Sources	rec. center sink, exterior						X	Drinking fountain by the lounge leaks. Plaza fountains could use cleaning.
Drinking Fountains		4			X			
Decorative Fountains	main plaza	3				X		
Spray Pools	N/A							

Conclusions: After meeting with residents, it seems as though everyone wants recycling bins in the park. Anne A. has volunteered to get in touch with the parks department and Charlie will explore the potential cost. A second concern is the southside parking lot. The matter should be discussed at the November meeting.

Barbara McCabe (center), parks coordinator for the Philadelphia Department of Recreation, meets with park volunteers.

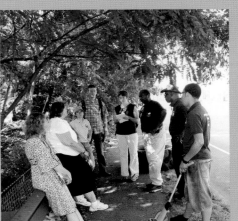

Recruiting Volunteers

Once your core group is established, invite the neighborhood to get involved. Host an event or workday in the park to attract them and let them know of all the ways they can participate.

T-shirts show your park pride.

Use volunteer sign-up sheets to collect names and contact information.

Cast a Wide Net

Post flyers in the park a few weeks before the event. Also distribute flyers to schools, religious institutions, and other neighborhood organizations. Post them in neighborhood gathering places like coffee shops, book stores, and libraries. Place information about your event in the community events column in the local newspaper.

In this early phase, it is imperative to have an open process. Don't make your group seem exclusive or give the impression that you're "taking over" the park. Instead, be responsive to the ideas and concerns of all the park's stakeholders.

Prepare a sign-in sheet before each workday. In addition to collecting names and contact information, have a space for people to express which projects interest them most or any special skills or resources they have to offer.

Once you have a list of volunteers assembled, create methods for keeping them informed of upcoming workdays and other items. Decide as a group whether this means weekly emails, a phone tree, or regular meetings.

It's important to be consistent without being overbearing. People only have so much time to give, so don't make being a park volunteer seem like a second job. Make it clear that people are free to choose their level of involvement. Maybe they are willing to show up on workdays, but not to attend meetings. That's okay, too. You'll want to convey that your group is committed to improving the park and appreciates volunteer assistance.

And while inclusion is important, don't let it slow down your group's progress. Occasionally people will disagree with the group, but you can't please all people all the time. Keep working toward your goals.

Targeted Recruitment

If you need a large number of volunteers for a big task, be strategic. Most schools have a service-learning requirement, and you may be able to work with a teacher to have an entire class come out for your workday. Or perhaps a local religious institution would devote a service day to the park. If there is a daycare or school that uses the park, they may be willing to ask parents to volunteer. Set up a table with information and a sign-up sheet at a neighborhood farmers market or flea market, or at the mall.

Host a Special Event

Park events are a great opportunity to recruit volunteers. Depending on your park's status, this could be something practical like a cleanup day or something fun like a concert or children's event. (See Chapter 5 for more on park programming.) Perhaps you could host a workshop on tree pruning or other useful skills. Whatever you choose, collect names and use the experience to gauge the enthusiasm of the neighborhood and the planning required for such events. Afterward, reflect on how you can improve on this initial event and expand upon it for a wider audience.

See the Resources section for helpful websites and references on working with volunteers.

Chapter 3: Growing the Park Group

Creating Successful Partnerships

No matter how dedicated, a group of volunteers cannot transform a park on its own. At the very least, you must establish a good working relationship with the owner of the park. To be successful, you will also need the collaboration of many other people, including park users; local businesses, schools, and religious institutions; and other stakeholders who stand to benefit from a better park.

By working together in partnership, your group can maximize its capacities, talents, and energy and accomplish much more than it could on its own. In the process you'll build a broader, longer-lasting base of support for your park as well as a stronger community.

"Working together toward a common goal, each partner can accomplish much more than any one person or organization could hope to achieve alone. The whole becomes greater than the sum of the parts."
– Joan Reilly, Senior Director, Philadelphia Green

The Landowner: Working with Municipal Governments

Before beginning any park improvement, you must first determine who owns the land. In most cases, this will be your local city government (although the principles outlined here are applicable to working with private landowners as well).

Your first step is to determine which agency or individual will best serve as the main contact for your park. The best way to start gathering this information is by visiting your city or town's website or calling the main government office. There are two basic approaches to park oversight. In some cities, governance of all parkland is centralized in one office. In others it is broken up by district or neighborhood. There also may be some hybrid of the two approaches. Find out what kind of oversight is at work in your city.

Begin by contacting either the individual responsible for your park or the decision-makers within a central agency. This will often be the district manager, public relations manager, or community affairs officer. Explain that your group is eager to improve your park and would like to explore ways that you can collaborate with the agency.

Start with the assumption that government employees are committed to serving the common good. Try to view the situation through their eyes. Park maintenance can be a thankless job. Many of the problems and challenges found in parks are the result of limited and shrinking dollars and staff to support the work. Find out the level of resources available for parks in your city. Is the agency you're dealing with understaffed and underfunded? What role can volunteers play? Be respectful and constructive in your interactions and imagine ways that partnerships can leverage additional support.

Each municipality has its own set of policies regarding the use of parkland. As you move forward, remember that it is in your group's best interest to adhere to regulations. Find out about procedures and permit requirements before launching any projects. Even a simple cleanup may require interaction with the city, as you will need to arrange for pickup of large amounts of trash. By following the rules, you will receive better service over the long run and lay the foundation for a mutually respectful partnership. You'll also avoid giving your local government a reason to ignore or deny your requests right off the bat.

Cities are usually responsible for at least a basic level of service on city-owned parkland, including mowing, trash pickup, major repairs, and infrastructure repair (light fixtures; benches; and "hardscaping," including sidewalks and paved surfaces). In most cases, volunteers should not be expected to perform that type of labor. In cash-strapped park systems, horticulture is often the first thing to go, so you might want to start out with a proposal for a volunteer garden project or tree planting. Be sure to get the proper permission beforehand. (See Chapter 4 for more on planting projects.)

Above all, do not begin with an adversarial stance. Find the common ground. Assume good intention and contact the appropriate people about your concerns. If those people are not available or responsive, take your concerns to the next level of authority, but work hard not to burn bridges along the way. You want to get the problem addressed and simultaneously build and improve your working relationships whenever possible.

Remember to express appreciation for work performed. The value of a simple thank you cannot be overstated.

Fostering Trust

In some agencies, you may encounter initial suspicion of volunteer labor. Employees may be afraid of losing their jobs to volunteers, that volunteers might expose shortcomings within the agency, or that employees will be unable to control the work done by volunteers. Your job is to demonstrate to the city or agency that your group will be an asset. Establish your trustworthiness by respecting their procedures and following through on your promises.

Building an Enduring Partnership

A strong partnership is built on a shared vision. To create that shared vision, each partner must be prepared to do as much listening as talking. At the very first meeting, find out what's most important to each partner. Before you make any requests, take the time to learn about the partner's interests, concerns, and limitations. Also ask about their dreams for what could be. Take the time to understand your partner's challenges and look for ways you might be of help. Understand that the most effective partnership is about more than the park; it's also about working together to improve the whole community.

As you develop the relationship, keep the conversation going and always acknowledge any assistance you receive from partners. Don't forget to invite your partners—early and often—to fun events as well as workdays. Make them feel valued and recognized and let them see the possibilities.

Celebration is a vital part of the process. Take the time to publicly acknowledge volunteers, city employees, financial backers, and other partners. Good food, music, and ceremony all add up to making partners feel valued.

A successful partnership requires a large upfront investment of time and effort, and it's not always easy. Each group or organization has its own perspectives, interests, and methods of accomplishing its goals. Working together requires commitment, patience, and persistence, as well as flexibility on the part of everyone involved to overcome the occasional setbacks. But collaboration creates its own energy and produces its own rewards.

By combining resources, partners can increase their capacities and talents. Together, they can not only tackle problems, they can also create a vision for a better park and a better community and turn that vision into reality.

It is important to thank your volunteers and acknowledge your partnerships.

Volunteers at Pretzel Park

A good partnership is based on mutual self-interest, so think about how an improved park advances the interests of those who use it.

Other Partners and Where to Find Them

In addition to establishing a good working relationship with your city government, it is also essential to bring in additional partners for your park. This creates a wider base of support and will help your cause as you lobby for more support from the city or seek funding from foundations and businesses.

To find partners, pay attention to who is using the park. A good partnership is based on mutual self-interest, so think about how an improved park advances the interests of those who use it or simply live or work near it. As part of your park inventory, create a "community inventory" or survey to identify neighborhood institutions, organizations, and businesses that use the park or are located nearby; these are your potential partners. Offer to take them on a tour of the park and show them how they will benefit from making it better.

Is there a daycare center or school whose children use the playground? A better park will give them a more inviting space for their kids to play, and they may be able to use it as an outdoor classroom. Nearby businesses will benefit from a better park in several ways: Cleaner, safer parks make people feel comfortable in the neighborhood and more likely to patronize the businesses there. An attractive park might be a place for employees to have lunch. A business that sponsors a park event can gain visibility and goodwill—and more customers— through your flyers and banners.

Keep in mind that potential partners offer a variety of resources, some financial and some not. Each partner brings different assets to the table, such as a base of willing volunteers, facilities, technical knowledge, or even 501(c)(3) status (see page 40). A school may be able to tap into its parent community for workday volunteers. A religious institution or community center might have meeting space for your group. A local restaurant may be willing to provide snacks for volunteers or for a public event in exchange for recognition. Local musicians might enjoy the chance to perform for the neighborhood. An environmental group or garden club might partner with you on cleanups or beautification projects.

One of the most important partnerships to pursue is one with your local elected officials, such as city councilpersons or state representatives. Find out if one of them has an office near your park. Arrange a meeting to discuss the needs of the park. Give them a tour of the park, invite them to events, and thank them for any assistance they provide. (For more on working with elected officials, please see the Advocacy section in Chapter 4.)

Look beyond your neighborhood as well. For example, a bank or corporation with a large customer or employee base in your city might be willing to fund a new playground or other park improvements. Public acknowledgement of its gift is invaluable, since the company will benefit from being seen as a good neighbor.

How to Say Thanks

There are as many ways to say "thank you" as your imagination can dream up. The important thing is to remember to acknowledge everyone who plays a part in making your park better.

Thank your supporters with a simple phone call, email, card, or note after a meeting or helpful conversation. Build time for celebration into your schedule of park activities; plan a fun event—not a meeting—and use it as an opportunity to thank volunteers, partners, funders, and city employees for their hard work and support. You can do this after completing a project or at the end of a year of keeping the park vibrant. Special accomplishments can be celebrated with ribbon cuttings and press conferences, and everyone who played a part, however small, should be invited and acknowledged.

Philadelphia Green holds an annual Party for the Parks, which includes all park groups as well as partners. This event is usually held at a restaurant and includes recognition of volunteers, partners, and supporters. A "Volunteer of the Year" award is given to one person from each park group. An "Above and Beyond the Call" award is presented to an especially hardworking member of city maintenance crews, and all staff is thanked and recognized.

Everyone who played a part, however small, should be acknowledged.

A Philadelphia Green Story
Saunders Park Shapes Up!

The small park behind the University of Pennsylvania's Presbyterian Medical Center was in need of a facelift. Once a well-used community space in the Saunders Park section of West Philadelphia, the park had fallen into disrepair while the University, which owns the land, held it for an undetermined future use.

Restoration of the park began with a partnership facilitated by Philadelphia Green that brought together several organizations based in the neighborhood, including the University of Pennsylvania Health System, the People's Emergency Center Community Development Corporation, Saunders Park Neighbors, and UC Green. They began to brainstorm ways to turn the park back into the vital neighborhood asset it once was.

From the first meeting, there was a momentum that could not be stopped. "When partners are that willing to invest in the community, things can really move," reflects Joan Reilly of Philadelphia Green.

Generous funders—Bank of America and the William Penn Foundation—helped make the vision a reality, equipping the park with some much-needed items. Café-style seating, a garden area, and even handy "doggie stations" with bags for disposing waste, have all enhanced the beauty of the park. "We also installed a giant, flowering urn to recreate what the park likely looked like decades ago," says John Ungar of the People's Emergency Center.

Saunders Park residents were elated by the improvements, as were the folks at Penn Presbyterian, whose staff now take breaks in the park. "We hope our employees, patients, and visitors will see the park as a respite where they can sit and relax during what may be a very difficult time," says Gary Ginsberg, assistant executive director of hospital facilities. "In addition, we saw this as an opportunity to embrace our community and help stabilize the neighborhood. Everyone benefits."

"When partners are that willing to invest in the community, things can really move."

– Joan Reilly
Philadelphia Green

Park advocates and government leaders meet to discuss parks.

Philadelphia Mayor Michael Nutter receives a check from Secretary Michael DiBerardinis (rear) of the Pennsylvania Department of Conservation and Natural Resources for six park projects.

COMMONWEALTH OF PENNSYLVANIA

Date June 14, 2008

$1,000,000

Pay to the order of

City of Philadelphia

For 6 park/rec projects

Edward G. Rendell
Governor Edward G. Rendell

Fundraising

Fundraising should be seen as an integral part of your park program. Why do you need to fundraise? To build a new playground; create a garden; build a tool shed; purchase trees, plants, mulch, supplies or equipment; pay for services such as concrete work, signs, or tree pruning; and pay costs associated with special events like concerts, flea markets, and film series.

Whether you're requesting donations from an individual or a business, fundraising is far simpler when a group is organized. Your group will need to agree on priorities and develop a clear, well-thought-out vision of what you want to accomplish. This can be communicated through literature (brochures, flyers, etc.) that explains your purpose and how the funds will be directed.

Grassroots Fundraising

Individuals

Don't be afraid to ask family, friends, and neighbors for contributions; the worst they can do is say no. If they cannot provide money, perhaps they will volunteer their time. Utilize direct mail or door-to-door canvassing. Keep a list of contributors and add their names to a potential volunteer file for a follow-up mailer.

Community Institutions

Start with organizations in your neighborhood such as religious institutions, colleges, parent-teacher organizations, and community groups (Kiwanis, garden clubs, etc.).

Local Businesses

Ask home and garden centers, hardware stores, print shops, supermarkets, and coffee shops for cash donations or in-kind services. Sometimes receiving donuts or tools can be as beneficial as a cash contribution.

Fundraising Events

Special events are a great way to raise money and generate publicity. These events can be as varied as a bake sale, community flea market, raffle, car wash, garden tour, silent auction, or concert. Fundraising events are also good opportunities for recruiting new volunteers.

Government Officials

Local government officials, such as city councilpersons, state representatives, and even members of Congress have access to funds that may be available for neighborhood projects. They can also be important connectors who can help facilitate relationships between your group and grant-making organizations.

Obtaining Grants

Grants are available from foundations; organizations; and city, state, and national agencies. Before approaching an organization for a grant, you must do some research. Grant-making organizations usually have specific areas of focus, and you must be sure that your project is a good fit. They may accept proposals only at certain times of the year, and you must follow their guidelines and meet all deadlines.

Tap into Business

Learn about corporations, banks, utility companies, fuel companies, and other industries prevalent in your city. Many corporations have charitable foundations, and their websites give their areas of interest and explain guidelines for applying for grants.

Most cities have a locally focused business journal, a newspaper that covers business affairs in your region. These journals also publish a "Book of Lists," which identifies philanthropic organizations operating in your area.

Visit your Local Library

Your library provides free access to online databases, as well as directories in print, where you can search for available grants. Many state-run databases listing foundations are now online. Your librarian can help you access these materials.

A National Resource for Grant Seekers

The Foundation Center (*http://foundationcenter.org*) is a national organization that maintains a comprehensive database of foundations all over the country. On their website you can search by foundations' areas of interest, and you can view tax filings for particular foundations, showing what grants they have made in past years and the amounts. The Foundation Center is also a valuable resource for learning about fundraising, offering books, courses, and other training materials.

The Foundation Center also offers a directory of "Cooperating Collections," free information centers within libraries, community foundations, and other nonprofit resource centers throughout the country. These provide a core collection of Foundation Center publications and supplementary materials and services in areas useful to grant seekers.

Leveraging Resources

Simply stated, "leveraging" is the process of using resources to gain more resources. In other words, money raised can be used to raise more money. If your organization or group secures a grant from a foundation or corporation, it serves as an important "stamp of approval" that will help you make your case as you solicit funds from others.

Two examples of leveraging tools are "challenge grants," and "matching funds." With a challenge grant, one grantor pledges money to your organization with the stipulation that the money will be granted only if your organization can raise a specified amount from other sources. A matching grant awards a specified amount for each dollar raised elsewhere.

For example, Foundation A may stipulate that it will award $500 dollars for every $1,000 received from other foundations. The thinking behind this type of grant is that it strengthens the organization by forcing it to broaden its base of support.

Leveraging applies not just to money, but also to other resources as well. "Sweat equity" can be used to leverage other support. For example, if your city government or a local foundation sees that people feel so strongly about improving parks that they will volunteer their time, this can convince them to commit more funds.

Documentation is key when making your case. Use statistics from park events and celebrations to bolster your case. As Peter Harnik of the Trust for Public Land says, "If we don't count, we don't count." Meaning that it's far easier to tout the park's success with accompanying data. Consider the number of people who use the park daily, the number of people who volunteer, or any other figures that will illustrate to potential supporters the value of your efforts.

Visible improvements are another important leveraging tool. They create excitement and encouragement that positive change is happening, and that can inspire others to help fuel the momentum in a variety of ways. The accomplishments of your group can help you attract other volunteers who want to be part of the action. The "in-kind" gifts you receive (such as snacks for an event donated by a local restaurant) may inspire other local operations to offer their services and have their name placed on your banners.

Basic Tips for Proposal Writing

When writing a proposal, follow the instructions precisely and adhere to deadlines. Funders may eliminate proposals that do not contain the necessary information or meet their guidelines. Pay attention to details including: margin size, number of pages, and the sequence of information.

Supplemental materials can add credibility to your application. Include supporting information from the following areas: project costs, letters of recommendation in support of the project, and any publicity that your group has received.

Here are some general questions often asked on grant applications:
- Who is applying for the grant? What is the group's mission?
- What is your group asking for? (Try to be as specific as possible.)
- How will your group accomplish the task? (Be as detailed as possible.)
- Who are the group's partners?
- What is the impact of this project on the community?
- How does your organization evaluate its projects?

Should your Park be a 501(c)(3)?

To solidify the identity of your friends group, you might want to register it as a 501(c)(3), a federally recognized charitable organization. This comes with many benefits, particularly making park-related expenses tax exempt. Navigating the sea of bureaucracy can be intimidating, so a park group should be well-defined before entertaining the prospect. But if you're serious about taking your fundraising to the next level, use the questions below to "test" your readiness.

- Would you like to solicit donations from the public?
- Is your group willing to devote time toward fundraising?
- Would you prefer to purchase items at a discount and not have to pay sales tax (or perhaps receive items free of cost from local merchants)?
- Does the nature of your park group potentially appeal to foundations or local businesses that provide grants to community service organizations?
- Does someone in the group have financial or other recordkeeping skills? If not, is someone willing to learn?
- Do you have people who might serve on a board of directors? Are you willing to relinquish some control over activities and funding to that board?
- Are you comfortable with the fact that, as a 501(c)3 organization, the financial affairs of your park group would be open to public scrutiny?

If you answered "yes" to all or most of these questions, you are ready to lay the groundwork for becoming a 501(c)3. Before proceeding, know that this process is time consuming. Also, filing fees will cost a few hundred dollars, but the real expense is hiring a lawyer or accountant to carry out the application process. Try to find someone who would be willing to do the work pro bono (for free); otherwise, budget accordingly.

An alternative to having your park group become a 501(c)3 is partnering with an existing organization that already has that status, such as a community development group or religious institution. By stepping under that organization's "umbrella," you may have to concede some control over decision-making and allocation of funds. However, the plus side is that the affiliation helps forge your group's identity and purpose while sharing some of the responsibilities.

Remember, a park group does not need to apply for 501(c)3 status, it's just one option. If your group is still "finding its legs," has modest goals, or can link up with an umbrella organization, it may not be worth the trouble. To learn more about the pros and cons, visit the IRS website at *www.irs.gov/charities/charitable/index.html.*

The Parks Revitalization Project
and Philadelphia Green

124

Pay to the
Order of   The City of Philadelphia

Date Dec. 6, 2007

$ 1,350,000.00

One million three hundred fiftythousand and ———————— 00/xx Dollars

Memo Park Group Volunteer Labor, 2007

The Park Volunteers

000123456 7809

The Value of Volunteer Time

The Independent Sector is a nonpartisan coalition of leaders from the U.S. charitable and philanthropic sector. Each year the group determines the estimated hourly value of volunteer time. In 2007, they deemed it to be $19.51 per hour. The purpose of this figure is to "help acknowledge the millions of individuals who dedicate their time, talents, and energy to making a difference."

At the end of each year, the Philadelphia Green Parks Revitalization Project tallies up the volunteer hours amassed in the past 12 months. That total, when multiplied by the Independent Sector's dollar value, is revealed at the celebratory Party for the Parks. There, park leaders present the figure on an oversized check to illustrate what volunteer time is worth. In 2007 that number was $1,350,000. Such an impressive sum can then be used as leverage for fundraising efforts.

Standing up for Parks: Advocacy

Park stewards must spread the word among the public, press, and city officials about the valuable benefits parks provide. Well-kept parks and green spaces improve the quality of life in city neighborhoods by offering respite from the urban environment, promoting social interaction, reducing crime, and improving health. A thriving park used and enjoyed by residents is a sign of a desirable neighborhood, attracting new residents, businesses, and investment. (See Chapter 1 for more on the benefits of parks.)

Unfortunately, parks are often a low priority when municipal budgets are tight. Local lawmakers need to be reminded that parks are wise investments that provide considerable returns. Parks have been shown to improve local economies by increasing property values and attracting investment. (A recent study by the Trust for Public Land demonstrates that Philadelphia's park system is worth more than $1.8 billion annually in revenue and savings.) Neglected parks, on the other hand, exacerbate neighborhood decline and often become a breeding ground for crime.

It is up to you and the group to be the voice of the park. To advance the park's agenda, reach out to three key groups: the public, the press, and the politicians.

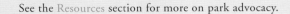

See the Resources section for more on park advocacy.

Open communication with volunteers is vital to your park's success.

Raise Public Awareness

Keep Volunteers Informed

Volunteers and residents of your neighborhood can be valuable advocates for your park. If there are upcoming legislative votes that impact parks, keep them informed of the issues and let them know what they can do, such as contacting their elected representatives. Pass out flyers or information on park cleanup days or post flyers in the park. Other methods of disseminating information include sending emails, writing articles for the local paper, creating a website, and establishing a phone tree.

Join your Neighborhood Association

Make sure that your park group is represented in local organizations such as the community development corporation or neighborhood association. These groups usually have established relationships with city and state representatives or other government officials. Have someone from your group attend meetings and place items on the agenda related to parks and open space. You can also use these meetings to enlist volunteers.

Join Forces with Other Activist Groups

Find other organizations whose interests dovetail with your own, such as environmental organizations, bicycling clubs, health advocates, neighborhood beautification groups, community gardens, and community development organizations. Work together to champion green spaces throughout your city. Support their causes as they support yours.

Enlist the Support of Elected Officials

Elected officials pay attention to what their constituents care about, so let them know that voters in their district care about parks. Enlist the support of your local, city, state, and federal representatives. Pay attention to legislative agendas, and speak up regarding the importance of funding for parks.

Use the Power of the Pen

Tips for writing letters to elected officials:

- Personal letters are most effective. The contents should be polite, informative, and concise.
- Spell the official's name correctly and include his or her correct title.
- Keep your letter to one typewritten page.
- State your purpose in the first paragraph. Keep it brief and stay with one topic or issue.
- Direct your approach to the legislator's committee assignments, interests, and background.
- If your topic is related to a particular bill, cite it by name and number.
- Be factual and support your position with information about the legislation and its effects on parks. Avoid emotional and philosophical arguments.
- If you are in opposition to a piece of legislation, say so, and then indicate the adverse effects it would have. Offer alternative approaches.
- Ask for your legislator's views and solicit their support.
- Be sure your name and address are legible.

Arrange a meeting

A personal visit with a member of your city council, a state official, or member of the U.S. Congress is an effective way to emphasize your interest in an issue or a piece of legislation.

Tips for face-to-face meetings with elected officials:

- Select a spokesperson and agree on the presentation.
- Make an appointment. State the subject of discussion, the time needed, and identify persons attending.
- Know the facts related to your position. Support your position with research and information.
- If you are discussing a particular bill, know the bill's title and number.
- Present the facts in a positive and concise manner.
- Relate the positive impact from the legislation and state the problems it corrects.
- If you are opposing legislation, highlight the negative impact. If possible, have an alternative approach.
- Leave accompanying fact sheets.
- Encourage questions and discussion.
- Ask the legislator for support. Thank the legislator for his or her time.
- Follow up the meeting with a thank-you note.

Pay attention to legislative agendas and speak up regarding the importance of funding for parks.

Introduce them to the Park

Invite your elected officials to park events. Take them on tours and introduce them to key people. Meet with them at strategic intervals to let them know the many ways the park helps their constituents and seek support for future projects.

Organize a Rally

If your city or town is considering legislation that affects parks, organize a rally. Be sure to invite well-informed speakers, including legislators who support your position.

Say Thanks!

If elected officials go to bat for your issue, be sure to let them know you appreciate their support. Send thank-you letters and invite them often to your events and celebrations.

Contact Advocacy Organizations

City Parks Alliance
(*www.cityparksalliance.org*)

The City Parks Alliance is a national organization comprised of parks leaders from across the country who work together to strengthen America's city parks. The organization was formed by park advocates who recognize the critical role parks play in the revitalization of our cities. The mission of City Parks Alliance is to create vibrant and healthy parks and green spaces that contribute to sustainable cities by organizing, facilitating, and nurturing a broad-based movement.

Philadelphia Parks Alliance
(*www.philaparks.org*)

The Philadelphia Parks Alliance works to mobilize community support, build coalitions, educate the public, and advocate for constructive change that will create a superior system of parks and open space in Philadelphia.

Meet the Press

Having a park group is great. Having a park group that's a vital and visible part of the community is even better. To advance your mission, become familiar with the staff of your local news outlets. Let them know about your group, your accomplishments, your concerns, and your immediate goals. Invite these press contacts to park events. If they don't take the bait, write your own story and submit your own photos. Don't be surprised if they end up on the front page.

Here are some tips for engaging the media:

Write Letters to the Editor

Writing a letter to the editor of your local newspaper is a good way to make your voice heard. Politicians pay attention to the editorial pages of newspapers to learn what their constituents think about a particular issue.

Tips for writing letters to the editor:

- Keep your letter brief; focus on two to three points at most.
- Whenever possible, relate your letter to a recent news article or to a relevant upcoming vote in the legislature.
- State the main point of your letter in the first or second sentence.
- If applicable, identify yourself as part of a group (member of a community organization, a parent, a business owner, etc.).

Invite Newspapers and TV Stations to Events

In the weeks before an event:

- Call around to reporters. Pitch your story so it sounds compelling and have all the necessary facts on hand (who, where, when, etc.). Let them know if any local VIPs will be in attendance.
- Prepare a press release or fact sheet that will serve as the reporters' framework for an article. Use numbers where applicable (i.e., 300 volunteers will plant 50 trees). Be sure to include contact information in case there are follow-up questions.
- If a newspaper has a regular listing of local events, find out the process for getting your event included.

At the event:

- Greet reporters, photographers, and camera operators when they arrive.
- Distribute the press release.
- Give the reporters "face-time" with the park leader or other noteworthy people. Remember, this doesn't have to be a celebrity, just a well-spoken person with an interesting, relevant story or opinion to share.
- Answer any questions.

After the event:

- Acquire printed stories and make copies for distribution among the park group, as well as to any funders and partners. If footage made the local TV news, show the segment at the next meeting.
- Evaluate the coverage. Did all the key message points come across? If not, how can you reframe future events?
- Send a brief thank-you note to your new media contacts. Some kind words may make them more likely to attend future park events.

Reach out to Radio Stations

Explore the programming of local radio stations. If a station has an interview program that covers community affairs, perhaps they would like to interview a knowledgeable park advocate or the leader of your park group, especially if there are current issues related to parks or open space in the news.

Let radio stations know about upcoming happenings in your park. Some locally run stations broadcast a "calendar of events." Sometimes a radio station will even broadcast from a community event. This mutually beneficial arrangement serves several purposes. For one, in exchange for promoting your park on-air, the radio station benefits from exposure through signage and interaction with volunteers. The radio station may even host contests and giveaways. Also, whether it's a workday or celebration, music makes everything more festive. Partner with a radio station that plays music everyone can enjoy.

The Friends of Smith Street Park

FOR INFORMATION, CONTACT:
Lana Bartmein, *lbartmein@email.com* or 555-555-5555

News Update: 10/01/2008

Fall Celebration Scheduled for October 17

Join the Friends of Smith Street Park on Saturday, October 17 from 8 am to 9 pm as they celebrate the fall harvest. An annual tradition dating back to 1991, the Friends Fall Festival features games, free food, hayrides, and other activities for the whole family.

Theodora Carlson, president of the Friends of Smith Street Park, says, "The Friends Fall Festival is the highlight of the season. In the past we've had as many as 1,000 New Townington residents drop by, and this year we hope to double attendance!"

Mayor Miguel Q. Ramirez is slated to kick off the opening ceremony, and hometown hero Constance O'Leary—winner of Talent USA—will sing the national anthem.

The Friends Fall Festival is sponsored by Insurance Bank Inc. and Caldero's Hardware Store. Refreshments will be provided by Shrimp & Stuff seafood restaurant and Venice Pizza Parlor.

Founded in 1987, the Friends of Smith Street Park is committed to making Smith Street Park a safe, fun place for New Townington residents of all ages. With an active membership of 30 volunteers, the Friends of SSP coordinate park cleanup days and community events. For additional information, please visit *www.smithparkfriends.com*.

How to Write a Press Release

The beginning or completion of a new park, the announcement of a new partnership, a park cleanup or planting, or any number of other park events can be an opportunity for media coverage. A good way to spread the word is through dissemination of a press release or media advisory.

The press release itself should be a mini story with the same structure as a news report. Start with a headline that will catch the eye of editors and news directors. It should clearly state the reason for the event and the reason readers and viewers will want to know about it.

The body of the press release should answer the basic journalistic questions: what, who, when, where, and why. The lead sentence or two should get to the point quickly and answer the first question, *what* is going on. Provide the exact time and date, the precise location of the park, and the site of the event within the park. In listing who will attend, provide correct spellings and full titles of participants and organizations. The details can be explained in a paragraph or two, but keep it concise and brief. Include contact names, phone numbers, and email addresses for more information.

Television, print, and new media all rely on visual aspects of a story, so use language that conveys what will be appealing to cameras, whether it is the park, the participants, or the activity involved.

After the press releases are sent out, follow up with phone calls to the editors, producers, or reporters. An extra push the day before the event is often very effective.

Chapter 4: Building a Better Park

Park Management

Park management means ensuring that your park is a clean, inviting, and safe space. It includes landscape management, maintenance, safety, crime prevention, and encouraging positive use.

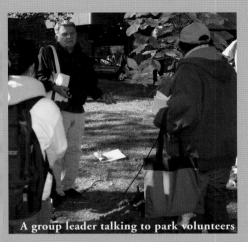
A group leader talking to park volunteers

Clean and Safe

Your first priority is making sure the park is safe and clean. Litter, broken benches, overgrown weeds, and graffiti send a message that the park is neglected and dangerous, keeping legitimate users away. Do all you can to make the park look better quickly, starting with picking up litter. If your park group cannot replace broken benches, remove them. Better to have no benches than unusable ones. As soon as possible, have your city agency or an arborist inspect and prune existing trees and remove dead or dangerous trees or branches.

Painting over graffiti helps discourage repeat incidents.

Safety, Crime, and Vandalism

- Communicate with the landowner to establish a clear understanding of whom to contact when emergencies arise, such as hazardous trees, downed power lines, or water-main breaks. Volunteer groups should not try to tackle these situations alone.

- Work with the landowner to repair damaged furnishings or playground equipment as soon as possible; remove any equipment that poses a hazard.

- If your park has a crime problem, such as drug-dealing, robberies, or vandalism, work with your local police and town watch organization and ask them to keep an extra eye on your park.

- Maintain a regular schedule of workdays and activities. Your group's presence in the park will help discourage crime.

- Be vigilant about graffiti. Removing it as soon as possible discourages repeat offenses over time.

- Encourage positive use of the park; plan activities that bring neighborhood residents into the park.

- When installing new plants, keep sightlines open. It's a good idea to keep the mid-zone (between 3 and 8 feet off the ground) open so you can see through.

- Place benches near light posts, so nighttime park users are visible.

- Secure park furnishings and use vandal-resistant bolts on signs and benches. If vandalism does occur, address it right away; remove, repair, or replace damaged equipment, broken branches, or plants as soon as possible.

Caring for your Park Landscape

General Maintenance

Maintenance is an essential component of park stewardship. Parks are meant to be used and enjoyed, but they quickly appear rundown if not properly cared for. Usually, the city or landowner maintains a regular schedule of mowing and trash collection. Determine which standard maintenance tasks are performed by the city or landowner and when. Learn the names of contact people for various aspects of park maintenance (plumbing, tree care, lighting, etc.) and establish good working relationships with them.

Workdays

Your group should establish a regular schedule of workdays to ensure a sufficient level of upkeep. Coordinate with the city to make sure large amounts of waste from workdays is removed promptly.

Having a regular, predictable workday schedule makes planning easier. Workdays should include a range of activities and should focus on two or three tasks, from simple cleanups and weeding to planting and mulching. Routine cleanup days make a big impact on your park's appearance. Major projects should be reserved for annual or seasonal large-scale workdays.

Workdays are an ideal opportunity to determine your park's needs. Is graffiti an issue? Is playground equipment damaged or unsafe? You can identify problem areas and address them at the next meeting. Workdays also help keep the group connected and foster communication.

Tasks for Workdays

Trash pickup

Cleaning up trash is one of the simplest ways to make your park look better, and it is an ongoing task. There are many ways to make it more enjoyable for volunteers. Have snacks, play music, or even divide the volunteers into teams and have them "compete" to see who collects more litter.

Watering

Work with the landowner to make sure there is an accessible water source for your park. Create a plan for watering newly planted trees and planting beds.

Composting

Begin a compost pile for your park and turn fall leaves, grass clippings, and garden refuse into free fertilizer. Spread compost on garden beds and on lawns. Compost must be turned periodically. Consult your local library for books on composting; contact your state Extension Service for workshops and educational materials; or *visit www.howtocompost. org*, as well as dozens of other websites, for helpful tips on composting.

A "how-to" workshop

Fun and Learning

In addition to workdays, schedule occasional educational activities, such as bird walks, lectures, or tree workshops, especially in the winter months, to keep interest high among your group. Bring in a horticulturist to demonstrate pruning techniques. Invite an ornithologist to discuss birds that may be spotted in your park. Many experts are happy to speak to groups for free. Check with local museums and nature organizations to see if they have a list of available speakers. (The PHS McLean Library maintains a list of speakers for the Philadelphia region.)

Adding Landscape Features

Each park landscape is different. The park's size, location, and usage patterns will all come into play as you develop a vision for your park. A master plan for your park should include a description of the park's landscape features, including plants and trees as well as hardscapes (sidewalks and other paved areas, buildings, and playgrounds), and will help determine your first steps (See page 62 for more on master plans).

If the park is in relatively good condition, without serious crime, vandalism, or litter problems, you'll want to begin focusing on ways to make the park even better, such as an enhanced entranceway, signage, or new trees and plantings.

A distinctive piece of artwork can become a signature feature of your park.

Trees

Once you are ready to enhance your park's landscape, it often makes sense to focus on trees first. Adding healthy trees is a great way to bring beauty to the park quickly, and trees are easier to maintain than flower beds and gardens. The task of planting and maintaining trees is also a good starting point for new volunteer groups. Your group can build its capacity by organizing planting days, tree inventories, and regular tree-care tasks.

Choose the Right Tree
Spring flowers and fall color may come to mind first, but it's important to consider all the pros and cons of different tree species. Before purchasing a tree, think about what kind of tree is most appropriate for the site. Consider overhead wires, amount of sunlight, soil pH, and drainage. Each tree species has specific requirements, and some are more tolerant of city stresses like road salts, compacted soil, and air pollution. Knowing your site will help you choose a tree that will thrive.

Ask yourself if the tree will be appropriate in 25 years. Imagine your tree in a planting site when the tree reaches it *mature size*. Can the site accommodate a large tree? Would a small tree, a columnar tree, or a wide-spreading tree suit the site better? Does the tree produce seeds, cones, or other droppings that might pose a problem in this location? Allow adequate spacing between trees based on their size at *maturity*.

For new plantings, select at least two-inch-caliper trees (the diameter of the trunk), since these are not as easily damaged as smaller saplings.

Water
Newly planted trees require one inch of rain per week or equivalent supplemental watering during the first two years after planting. Be sure you have a plan in place to provide adequate water for new trees. When watering, the golden rule is "water weekly and deeply." Allow 10 to 15 gallons of water to seep slowly into the tree pit; watering too fast will cause the water to flow off the tree pit. It's best to use a trickling hose or five-gallon bucket with holes. You can also use a Treegator®, a large plastic bag that zips around the tree trunk. When filled, it delivers water slowly and evenly directly to the root system of a newly planted tree or shrub with no run-off or evaporation. Discontinue watering when the ground freezes. Start again in the spring when tree buds swell and sprout new leaves.

Mulch
Use mulch around trees and on planting beds to conserve moisture and discourage weeds. Mulch creates a boundary around trees and shrubs, making it less likely that they will be damaged by lawnmowers and other equipment. Apply mulch evenly at a depth of two inches. Do not pile mulch around the trunks of trees or shrubs because it traps moisture and encourages disease. Keep mulch at least two to three inches away from trunks and woody stems (the mulch layer should look more like a donut than a mountain). PHS recommends dark brown double-shredded hardwood-bark mulch. Rake and replenish mulch annually.

More about Trees

For tree-planting instruction, please view the demonstrations on the accompanying DVD for this manual or watch the videos on the PHS website at *www.pennsylvania horticulturalsociety.org*.

Also, see the Resources section for more information on tree care.

Pruning

Tree pruning falls into two categories:

Major tree pruning involves removing large branches from mature trees, as well as tree removal. Pruning tree branches beyond the reach of a hand-held pole pruner requires a professional. This work will often be performed by city or landowner. If you need to find a professional arborist, visit the website of the International Society of Arboriculture (*www.isa-arbor.com*). Ask for credentials, insurance verification, and references. Choose the contractor in whom you have the most confidence. Make sure the contractor has obtained the necessary permits from the city or landowner.

Minor tree pruning is removing *dead, damaged,* and *diseased* branches (the "three Ds"). To keep healthy trees and shrubs looking their best, your group can learn basic, feet-on-the-ground pruning techniques. Hand pruners, pruning saws, loppers, and pole pruners are some of the common tools used for minor pruning. Learning basic pruning skills is worth the time invested, as healthy trees can make a big difference in the appearance of your park.

Why prune?

- **Safety: to remove low limbs in the pedestrian right-of-way, weak limbs that may fall, and those growing into power lines**
- **Appearance: to enhance tree shape (only advisable for young trees)**
- **Health: to remove dead, diseased, and damaged branches**

When to prune

- **Anytime there are dead, diseased, and damaged branches**
- **Late winter: before leaf buds open**
- **Fall to spring: when there are no leaves**
- **Mid summer: once new shoot growth becomes woody**
- **Do not prune a recently transplanted tree.**

Fertilizing

Never fertilize a newly planted tree. Wait at least one year for the tree to become established. Then look for visible foliage symptoms to see if fertilizers are needed. Fertilizing will not solve problems caused by inadequate sunlight or water, air pollution, plant diseases, or insect attack. The young sapling, the mature healthy tree, and the declining tree have different needs.

To determine if the tree needs fertilizer, observe the leaf color. Unusual yellowing, especially between the veins, may indicate a specific nutritional deficiency. Notice if the old or new leaves are affected. Consult an arborist regarding a mature tree in trouble. A soil test from the tree pit will determine the fertilizers needed. (In Pennsylvania, test kits are available for a fee from Pennsylvania State University's Cooperative Extension at 215-560-4167.)

Newly planted trees require one inch of rain per week or equivalent supplemental watering during the first two years after planting. Be sure you have a plan in place to provide adequate water for new trees.

Conduct a Tree Inventory

A tree inventory is a complete assessment of your park's tree population. Enlist the support of an arborist or knowledgeable volunteer to conduct the survey or to guide your group through the process.

Coordinate your efforts with the agency or person responsible for the trees in your park. Be sure to follow protocol and space recommendations.

Usually, the location of trees is pinpointed on a map of the park, and an accompanying checklist describes the species, size, and condition. The inventory will help you zero in on priority maintenance and identify dead trees and hazardous limbs or branches that should be targeted for pruning or removal. It will also locate potential sites for new trees. Finally, an inventory helps formulate an action plan and helps you estimate costs for tree planting and care.

Trees Cost Money

You may need to hold a fundraising event or seek donations to pay for plants, fertilizer, and soil. Local plant retailers may be willing to donate material or give your group a discount on large purchases. See Chapter 3 for more on fundraising.

Go Gold!
www.goldmedalplants.org

The PHS Gold Medal Plant Award program promotes trees, shrubs, and woody vines of outstanding merit. These plants are evaluated and chosen for their superb eye-appeal, performance, and hardiness in the growing region of Zones 5–7. Many Gold Medal plants are also hardy in a broader geographic range.

Planting Beds and Gardens

A Word on Gardens

Flower gardens add charm and beauty to any park and can be a source of pride, particularly when placed at the entrance to your park. But keep in mind that garden beds require extensive care and upkeep, including planting, weeding, watering, dividing, mulching, and more. When considering whether to establish a garden, be realistic about the capacity of your group to maintain it. Is there enough interest to sustain a garden through spring, summer, and fall?

If you decide to create a garden or planting bed, first confer with the landowner. Then, work with a horticulturist, garden designer, or knowledgeable volunteer to devise a pleasing, practical plan that will add beauty throughout the year and can be maintained by your group. After planting, create a seasonal schedule for maintenance to keep the garden looking its best.

If you decide to create a garden or planting bed, wise selection of plants and proper placement will make a big difference in your park's appearance. When adding new plants, consider their growing needs before you make your selection. Also consider your local climate, light conditions, and water availability.

Garden beds are beautiful but require a lot of maintenance.

Annuals and Perennials

Annuals are plants that complete their life cycle in one growing season. Perennials are plants that go dormant over the winter, but their root systems remain alive underground and sprout new growth each spring.

Know your Zone

Before you plant, be sure the plants you choose will survive in your climate. Consult the U.S. Department of Agriculture Plant Hardiness Zone Map to identify which Zone your city is in. The map gives the range of annual average minimum temperatures in each Zone. Plant tags and mail-order catalogs usually indicate the Zone for which the plant is suitable.

For example, plants that are "hardy for Zone 6" (Philadelphia's Zone), can survive winter temperatures as low as minus 10 degrees Fahrenheit. Most basic gardening books contain this map. The website of the United States National Arboretum has an online, clickable zone map indicating temperature ranges down to individual counties (*www.usna.usda.gov/Hardzone/ushzmap.html*).

A Few Considerations for Park Plantings

Location

If you are going to invest time and energy into creating and maintaining a garden, choose the location with the most impact. A lovely garden planting at the entrance to your park, especially if the entranceway has been renovated, draws visitors into the park and can be a point of pride for your entire neighborhood. An eye-catching display will help build enthusiasm for additional park improvements. Other high-profile locations may be near sitting areas where visitors can enjoy the view or around central fountains or other features.

Light

Observe the light conditions in possible planting areas. Determine whether the site receives direct sunlight for most of the day (six hours or more, "full sun"), part of the day (part shade), or is completely in shade all day. Select plants according to their light needs.

Soil

Heavy clay soil or hard, compacted soil will need to be amended before planting can begin. Dig deep to loosen the soil and mix in compost, peat moss, or good-quality topsoil before planting. Remove large rocks and weeds.

Maintenance

Choose low-maintenance plants when possible. Plants native to your region are often good choices.

Water Conservation

Even if your park has a reliable water source, consider drought-tolerant plants and native plants that require less water. This not only conserves water, but also frees volunteers to spend time on other park improvements. Also, drought-tolerant plants survive better during dry spells.

Massing

Find one plant or shrub that you like and plant a lot of it, rather than a variety of plants. This planting style is easier to maintain.

Beware of Thorns

While roses and hollies are lovely, thorny and prickly plants are difficult to weed around. They also catch and hang onto trash such as plastic bags.

Playground Safety

Don't grow plants with thorns or poisonous plants near playground areas.

Trees

Areas immediately next to trees are not the best places for new plantings, since tree roots can make this difficult and flowers and shrubs will compete with the tree for nutrients and water.

Increase your Garden Know-How

An excellent book for all-around gardening advice is *The Garden Primer* by Barbara Damrosch. See the Resources section for more books and helpful websites on gardening.

For detailed information on sustainable lawn-care, including recommended varieties of grass, visit *www.sustland.umn.edu/maint/maint.htm.*

Grass

Open green lawns are one of the most inviting features of a well-managed park. Regular mowing is usually performed by the city or landowner. But keeping the grass looking its best requires more than simply mowing. Heavily used turf requires occasional *fertilization*, *reseeding*, and *aeration*.

Sustainable practices are transforming the care of turf. Maintaining a healthy lawn does not have to involve the use of harmful chemical fertilizers and herbicides. Learn about *sustainable turf care* and work with the city or landowner to encourage better lawn-care practices.

Selection

There are many varieties of turf grass available. Many, such as fescues, stand up much better to heavy foot traffic than the more widely used Kentucky blue grass.

Mowing

In most cases, your city or town is responsible for regular mowing of grass. Grass should be kept at a height of three to three-and-a-half inches, and no more than one-third of the grass blade's height should be removed at one time. The shade of taller grass discourages weed growth. Grass clippings should be left on the ground to decompose, supplying nitrogen to the turf.

If a portion of your park space is used as a playing field, the grass should be shorter than that of passive use spaces. This is especially true of sports that require a ball to roll, chiefly soccer. Communicate with those who perform the mowing and express your wishes in a friendly way.

Compost

About once each year, top-dress the lawn with compost (apply a sprinkling of compost and rake it evenly over the grass) and add more grass seed. This helps fill in empty spots, discourages weed growth, and nourishes the roots.

Aeration

Yearly aeration of the turf improves the lawn over time by encouraging a healthy root system. Aeration means poking small holes in the soil to allow air circulation. Mechanical tools are available to make this job easier.

Hardscapes, Playgrounds, and Furnishings

In your park inventory or survey, take note of the condition of "hardscapes" (sidewalks, plazas, game courts and other paved areas) and furnishings such as buildings, benches, lighting, and playgrounds. If your park needs new hardscapes or furnishings, you must consult with the city government or landowner. There may be city standards for furniture, and the city will choose an experienced contractor for design and installation. Invest in high-quality, sturdy items that can withstand heavy use. Your master plan should include a vision for new furnishings and hardscapes. (See page 62 for more on master plans.)

An attractive entrance can dramatically improve your park's appeal.

A Philadelphia Green Story
The Rebirth of Carroll Park

For years Doris Gwaltney of West Philadelphia was dismayed by the condition of her local green space, Carroll Park. With no one to look after it, the site was unsafe and attracted illegal activity. With the assistance of the Pennsylvania Horticultural Society's Philadelphia Green program, Doris and her neighbors decided to take matters into their own hands.

Beginning in the summer of 1997, Carroll Park experienced a rebirth as residents organized a series of workdays. They painted benches, planted trees, and removed invasive plants. "At our first cleanup day we had about 60 people," Gwaltney recalls. "We swept, picked up trash and glass, painted benches, and painted over the layers of graffiti on the shed. At the end of that day, we could stand in the center of the park and really feel that Carroll Park was on its way back."

As beautiful as the park looked, those involved knew it was a short-term victory without continued upkeep. To protect her investment, Doris decided to pick up trash every Monday afternoon at four o'clock. Regardless of rain, snow, or extreme heat, Doris was there in Carroll Park, proving her commitment. Soon a handful of neighbors pitched in as well, and now, years later, a group still convenes every Monday at four to clean up Carroll Park. Once a month, they tackle larger chores.

"If Doris and her group stop coming out here, in a matter of time the park will revert back," says Joan Reilly, senior director of Philadelphia Green. "Folks like Doris are green champions for their communities."

Doris Gwaltney

The Master Plan: A Road Map for a Great Park

What is a master plan? A master plan is a comprehensive planning document that guides the physical development of a landscape. The plan outlines all aspects of the park, including trees; planting beds; other landscape features; sidewalks, courts, and other "hardscapes;" and topography.

A master plan is different from a park inventory, an early step in which a group assesses the existing state of the park (see page 20). A master plan is focused on the future and what a park could be. A newly formed group should begin with a small project, such as a cleanup or tree planting, to build cohesiveness and capacity before drafting a master plan.

A master plan should be completed before any major park improvements are begun. It is an extremely valuable tool that will serve as a road map for turning your dreams into reality. It spells out your group's shared vision for the park and lays out a long-term strategy for achieving your goals in a systematic way.

Why You Need a Master Plan

A master plan will determine the assets of your park, as well as its limitations. It will encourage logical decision-making and will help you set priorities for improvement projects. A plan will set a schedule of phases for completion of projects, based on priorities and resources, and estimate the costs for each project and phase.

Without a plan, park projects are piecemeal and may result in costly "mistakes." Even if your park is in relatively good condition, a master plan will help you ensure its long-term sustainability. For example, perhaps your park has large, mature trees. Some of them may be nearing the end of their life expectancy and you need to think about "succession planting"—installing new trees now to replace older ones as they die off.

Having a master plan can help you mitigate conflicts and balance the needs of all park users. For example, your master plan can include a dog run or other dedicated areas for dog walkers separate from children's play spaces. You can also designate certain areas of the park for active use (ball-playing, etc.) or passive use (quiet sitting areas with benches).

The process of creating a master plan is a great opportunity to engage the whole community—your group, the city agency, park users, the public, and all key stakeholders—and invite people to share their desires and concerns for the park.

Finally, a master plan is an excellent fundraising tool. Frequently, funders want to know exactly what they are putting their money into, and a master plan gives them detailed information. A plan serves as a menu of sorts; you can show it to a funder and ask them to support one distinct aspect, such as a single project or phase. Funders also like knowing their investment can be "leveraged," with other improvements funded by other organizations. Furthermore, a master plan demonstrates that the group is organized and reliable, and it makes a project look like a good investment. Your master plan should include one or two "early-action" projects that can be completed relatively quickly. These build excitement and momentum and can attract new partners and/or funding sources to your park.

Before You Begin

When embarking on a master plan, you must work with the city agency or landowner of the park. Master plans are documents that create an agreed-upon plan between the community and the city agency, so their involvement is essential. This will ensure that specific city standards for construction and park maintenance are integrated early in the process. Moreover, the city agency is an essential partner that can bring resources and expertise to the table.

Creating a Master Plan

Hire an Expert

In most cases, a master plan is completed by a landscape architect or planner. Ask for recommendations from your city agency, a landscape-based nonprofit organization (such as PHS), or any organization that has conducted landscape improvements. Make sure to select a professional who has completed similar projects, and that the person is a good fit for your group.

Some foundations and government agencies, such as the Pennsylvania Department of Conservation and Natural Resources, provide grants for master plans. Alternatively, look for ways to get professional assistance at no cost. Philadelphia is fortunate to have the Community Design Collaborative, an organization that offers design assistance to nonprofits. Investigate your local nonprofit community for similar organizations.

Engage the Community

Plan a meeting or series of meetings that include your group, the landscape architect, and interested members of the community to brainstorm ideas for the park. Choose a facilitator and someone to record answers on a flip chart. Have a clear agenda. Begin the discussion by having attendees answer the following questions:

- **What do you like about the park?**
- **What are your concerns about the park?**
- **What are your suggestions for improving the park?**
- **What are your hopes and dreams for the park?**

Afterward, pass out small stickers and ask people to place a sticker next to their highest priority items. Review the information as a group and allow time for comments and questions.

You can also gather information by passing out surveys to park users. Surveys can gather detailed information about how people use the park. Please see the Resources section for tools and references on effective community engagement.

Evaluating a bed of plants

An informal meeting in a park

Design Assistance

Based in Philadelphia, the Community Design Collaborative offers preliminary design assistance to nonprofits (*www.cdesignc .org*, see Resources). The Collaborative meets with nonprofits at the beginning of a project, develops a scope of services to fit their needs, and recruits design professionals to provide the services pro bono. More than a dozen parks in Philadelphia have received designs through the Community Design Collaborative, and those designs were used as springboards to major improvements.

Your Master Plan Should Include:

Site Plan/Topographical Survey

A survey is a detailed record of the location, dimensions, landscape features, location of utilities, and all contents of your park. A survey is completed by a trained surveyor or engineer. The survey will result in a detailed map of your park. Check with your city agency or landowner; they may already have one for the site that can be used.

Project Brief

A project brief is a description of the desired outcomes of the master plan. The brief should document the client's (i.e. park group) needs and goals and include items such as desired activities, open space needs, material preferences, budgetary constraints, etc.

Site Analysis and Evaluation

A survey tells you simply what is in the park. A site analysis examines each element of the park and helps determine opportunities and constraints. This is a crucial step; the amount of site research and understanding will determine the ultimate success of your master plan. A site analysis includes:

Climatic Analysis: Wind patterns, sun/shade diagrams, and rainfall

Landform Analysis: Slope analysis, site orientation, and drainage patterns

Physical Analysis: Soil type and condition; geology; wetlands; vegetation; habitats; "view shed" analysis (what can be seen from inside the park—desirable as well as undesirable views); and positive and negative attributes

Current Usage Analysis: Pedestrian circulation patterns, activity zones and activity types, congregation points, and community surveys

Historic Site Usage Analysis: History of site, including foundations, septic systems, pollution, etc.

Infrastructure Analysis: Utilities (availability and location of gas, water, sewer, electric lines); public transportation routes; vehicular circulation; parking; and lighting

Adjacent Use Analysis: Neighboring land use and demographics

Regulatory Analysis: Building regulations; historic-site regulations; set-backs (distances from property lines where building is allowed); property lines; rights of way/easements; and ADA requirements (compliance with the Americans with Disabilities Act)

A Master Plan for Philadelphia

The City of Philadelphia is developing a comprehensive open space plan for the entire city. GreenPlan Philadelphia will help provide a long-term, sustainable roadmap for using, acquiring, developing, funding, and managing open space throughout the city. The plan will include an inventory of the natural resources and open spaces, funding strategies for implementation, an assessment of the costs and benefits of open space, and evaluation tools. For more information, please visit *www.greenplanphiladelphia.com.*

Proposed Improvements

- **Detailed maps and drawings of potential park improvement projects that reflect your group's shared vision**

- **A written description of proposed improvements**

- **Projects grouped into phases**

- **Cost estimates for each project and phase**

- **A list of "next steps" required for meeting your goals**

Note: A master plan will *not* include construction documents. These are technical documents that will be required before any construction can begin.

Once the master plan is complete, the work has just begun! It is only through the efforts of your group that the vision will become a reality. A master plan is effective only if it is implemented and faithfully followed. At the same time, a good master plan is flexible; it can be modified when necessary to adapt to changing circumstances.

What is a Landscape Architect?

In its broadest sense, landscape architecture deals with design of the open space between buildings, including everything from perceiving and experiencing the space to the plants, trees, pathways, and other landscape elements that fill the space. Landscape architects are adept at working at many different scales, from residential to regional.

A landscape architect (LA) usually holds an undergraduate and/or graduate degree in landscape architecture. Landscape architects are generally knowledgeable about ecology, geology, hydrology, horticulture, grading, stormwater management, construction practices, site analysis, and best landscape management practices. Most LAs can perform any or all of the following tasks: site analysis, conceptual design, design development, construction documentation (including written specifications and bid documents), construction and installation oversight, and monitoring of plants during the guarantee period. Landscape architects have a wide range of knowledge, but not all LAs are experts in all areas of the discipline.

A registered landscape architect (RLA) has passed a state licensing exam. While a non-registered landscape architect may be able to perform most of the tasks outlined, construction documents must be *sealed* by an RLA for liability reasons and for permitting in most cases. If your project is not going to the construction document phase, an RLA may not be necessary. Depending on the type of project, the seal of a professional engineer may be acceptable or preferable. You should research potential LAs for your project and search for a good match between the type of work and the experience and expertise of the designer.

To find a landscape architect or for more information, visit the website of the American Society of Landscape Architects (ASLA) at *www.asla.org*.

A master plan is usually completed by a landscape architect and planner working closely with the park group.

The Workday

Regular workdays are an ideal opportunity to ensure the upkeep of your park, maintain communication among group members, and identify any problems that need to be addressed.

Celebrate your park group's achievements with a group photo. Then send copies to all the members.

Volunteers receive instructions on a planting technique.

Planning Ahead

Those planning the workday should meet at least a month beforehand to start preparing. From the outset it's imperative to know what you hope to accomplish— use your park inventory (see page 20) to help set priorities. The larger the event, the more planning is required.

Set the date and decide how many volunteers you'd like to have, how you're going to generate enthusiasm for the day, and what tools and supplies you'll need to meet your goals. The devil is in the details, so think things through.

What's most important is ensuring that there's enough work for all the volunteers, even if more people arrive than you anticipate. There's nothing worse than having people stand around with nothing to do. If volunteers feel uninvolved or neglected, it's doubtful they'll attend future events. This can be avoided by dividing the volunteers into teams and assigning each team a specific task (raking, mulching, etc.).

Each team should have a leader, but more importantly, there should be someone who supervises the entire event. This person's sole responsibility is to stay on schedule and keep people happy and busy.

When it comes to large-scale workdays, park leaders should serve as hosts. Much like at a dinner party, a host makes people feel welcome, ensures things run smoothly, and is the "go-to" person if there are questions. Leaders should be highly visible and wear bright clothing (or at least a distinguishing hat, scarf, or bandana).

At some point, likely at the beginning or end of the day, gather the group together and recognize their contribution. Perhaps let them know more about your park and the park group—this is not only a recruitment pitch, but it makes the volunteers feel connected to the work.

Throughout the day, keep tallies on what's getting accomplished. In the future, when you're looking to attract sponsors or leverage resources, it helps to have hard data to support your claims. For instance, it's more compelling to say "150 volunteers planted 42 trees," than "lots of volunteers planted a few dozen trees."

It's never too early to start volunteering.

Resources and Setup

As committed as you are to the park, remember that you don't own the property. Check with the city or landowner early in the process to ensure no other events are planned for that day. Consider how and when the trash will be removed; after all, it can't stay on the curb for days. Contact the municipality and see what arrangements can be made.

Also get the landowner's permission if you intend to make major upgrades to the site, such as planting trees or installing garden beds. (Documentation keeps everyone organized. Follow regulations, get a permit, and do so well in advance.) Also tell the police department if you anticipate a lot of traffic or if you'd like them to block off certain roads.

Locate utility lines. This is particularly important when planting trees or shrubs close to the street. Pennsylvania residents can contact the Pennsylvania

Resident One Call System; its purpose is to prevent damage to underground facilities by promoting safety and providing communication networks among designers, excavators, and facility owners. Visit *www.pa1call.org* to learn more. Other states have similar services.

Water is crucial for planting days. Contact the city and ask about gaining access to a fire hydrant. A "bucket brigade" is a lot of work, but it's one solution. In short, protect your plant investment by providing enough water. (And be sure to have a maintenance plan for the weeks ahead. New plantings require lots of care, so follow through.)

People may need to use the restroom and wash their hands. If the park doesn't have a permanent facility, look into renting portable toilets for large events. If members of the park group live nearby, perhaps they'll consider making their bathrooms available to volunteers.

Don't Let Volunteers Go Hungry

Don't underestimate the importance of refreshments. A bag of chips—or even better, a healthy snack like fruit—can go a long way in making volunteers feel welcome and cared for.

Always have an abundance of drinking water available, especially on hot summer days. If supplies run low, know where you can get more.

Most people enjoy a cup of coffee and a donut in the morning, so have some available when volunteers arrive. (Hot chocolate or cider is a good alternative for younger volunteers.) Be sure to have all the necessary accessories, such as cream, sugar, cups, lids, stirrers, etc.

Sponsors

If your park doesn't have an existing long-term partner, perhaps a local business would agree to sponsor a workday. Whether the business donates funding or the manpower of employees, make sure the contribution is recognized.

Identify the corporate contact person and provide him or her with what's needed to make the workday a success. Both the park and the business benefit from good press, so get in touch with local news outlets and see if there's an inexpensive way to get signs and T-shirts printed.

For larger projects, consider planning an opening and/or closing ceremony. Have the emcee give a nod to the sponsor; perhaps invite the business owner or CEO to make a short speech. Also include local politicians in the action. Invite them to stop by and say a few remarks.

Children

They may be small, but children make great volunteers. When planning the day's chores, designate those that are appropriate and safe for youth. If applicable, obtain kid-sized tools. Because children need extra instruction and supervision, perhaps someone from the group can act as their coordinator. (For more information, see the youth section in Chapter 5.)

Dress

Let volunteers know beforehand what they should wear to the workday (This can be done through email, a phone tree, flyers, etc.). Think of the specific conditions of the park and how they affect the dress code. For instance, suggest volunteers wear long pants if poison ivy is present. It never hurts to reinforce what may seem obvious, such as comfortable, sturdy shoes. If the sun is strong or the park is wooded, advise people to wear a hat, sunscreen, and bug repellent.

Most importantly, each volunteer needs a pair of work gloves for safety and sanitation reasons. You never know what you will find when picking up refuse. Even if you ask volunteers to bring a pair of gloves from home, have plenty on hand for those who will inevitably forget.

Identify what's needed to make the workday a success. For larger projects, consider planning an opening and/or closing ceremony.

Tools and Supplies

In regard to tools: the larger it is, the fewer you need. For instance, if bulbs are to be planted, nearly each person will need a trowel. Items like hedge clippers and full-size shovels are typically less in demand. Contact your department of recreation or parks department to see if you can borrow tools for the day.

If the tools belong to your group, paint the tool handles in a bright color so they are easier to find. Or mark all tools with tape labels that denote where they belong. It's good to keep a log of who supplied what.

At the end of the day have at least one person make rounds to make sure all tools are picked up. You will need to accept the fact that tools will disappear and that, ultimately, it is out of your control.

Other must-haves include:
- **First-aid kit**
- **Endless supply of trash bags**
- **Nametags**
- **Hand sanitizer**
- **Sign-in sheet: These volunteers could be future group members, so collect their contact information.**

Safety

Safety should always be the top priority. It's strongly advised that power tools are not used for workdays, but if you must, conduct a safety seminar first and have goggles available.

Let people (especially children) know what is not supposed to be picked up when collecting trash: syringes, broken glass, etc. If needles are found, alert the authorities so that they can be safely disposed of. Also let the volunteers know of any poisonous plants that could be growing in the park, such as poison ivy. Ask around; perhaps a member of the park team can identify plants. (If some people are uncomfortable dealing with poison ivy, be considerate and find another role for them.)

Ticks are a hazard when working in woody areas. At the end of the day, remind volunteers to thoroughly check themselves for ticks when they get home.

How to Identify Poison Ivy

Poison ivy is best known for its stalks of three divided leaves. The leaves alternate along the stem, which sometimes feature gray-white berries. In the spring, poison ivy has a red hue that changes to green in summer. Like many plants, poison ivy has orange, yellow, and red leaves in fall.

Poison ivy grows up tree trunks or creeps across the ground. In certain conditions poison ivy can even grow to resemble a shrub; this makes it difficult to identify in winter when there are no telltale leaves. If poison ivy is present in your park, it's best to let professionals dispose of it. Notify the city or landowner.

Web Resources:

http://mdc.mo.gov/nathis/plantpage /flora/poivy/

www.poison-ivy.org/html/summer1.htm

A Philadelphia Green Story
Wonderful Workdays in Philadelphia

Although park maintenance is a year-round commitment, two days in particular highlight Philadelphia Green's devotion to the cause. The annual Spring Into Your Park is a citywide cleanup effort. In 2008 the event welcomed 2,000 volunteers who collected countless bags of trash and planted thousands of annuals and perennials in parks across the city.

Each October, the Fall For Your Park event inspires hundreds of volunteers to congregate at a specific park for a day of intensive renovation. This occasion encourages networking among greening advocates as they pitch in at a site outside their own neighborhoods.

The Philadelphia Department of Recreation and Fairmount Park partner with Philadelphia Green on these events. Corporate sponsors also play a valuable role.

While such large-scale cleanups may seem overwhelming to a new park group, remember, the Philadelphia Green parks project started small, too. By building on the goodwill generated by parks, the events have grown each year.

Seasonal Workday Activities

SPRING
- Plant spring flowers, such as lilies and daffodils.
- Plant trees.
- Clean out beds and mulch.
- Paint park buildings.
- Remove graffiti.
- Lay grass seed.
- Cut back plants and ornamental grasses.
- Clean statuary.
- Empty gutter systems (not just in the park, but around it).

SUMMER
- Prune bushes and trees.
- Pull weeds.
- Water newly planted flowers and trees.
- Place gator bags on trees.
- Perform general maintenance.

AUTUMN
- Plant perennials and spring bulbs.
- Plant trees.
- Winterize plants.
- Rake and remove leaves.
- Cover playground equipment.
- Divide plants.
- Turn off water sources so pipes don't freeze.

WINTER
- Plant trees (until the ground freezes).
- Plan for the new season.
- Clean up trash and litter; monitor for problems.

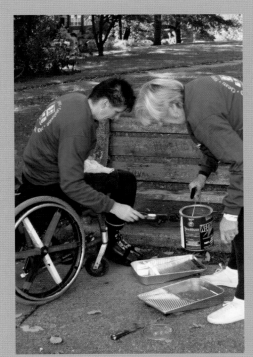

Workday Roles

Many hands make light work, so it's great to have lots of volunteers show up on the workday. But in order for things to run smoothly, each person must have a clear and pre-defined role. The following are suggested job descriptions to make certain the day is a success.

Workday Supervisor:
Oversees the operation from start to finish. Long before the event, this individual must plan the registration system, draft a workday schedule, and assist with the creation of the team list. Must also coordinate the sub-coordinators.

On the day of the event, the workday supervisor oversees the proceedings and recognizes the volunteers' efforts by providing refreshments and offering encouragement.

Afterward the workday supervisor sends thank-you notes to partners, sponsors, and volunteers and sets up a phone list of participants for future reference.

Publicity Coordinator:
Contacts local media (radio stations, television networks, and newspapers) weeks before the event to generate buzz and secure press coverage. When the day arrives, has prepared press releases for the media and is attentive to their questions and needs. Has a fully charged cell phone at his or her side at all times.

Registration Coordinator:
Responsible for the set-up and breakdown of the registration table (and getting the table to and from the park). Assigns volunteers into teams, keeping friends together when possible. Distributes handouts and other materials.

Food Coordinator:
Acquires and distributes snacks and beverages. Provides paper products and a serving table, and makes sure the hungry masses don't leave horrid messes.

Tool Coordinator:
Brings the necessary equipment to the site and provides it to the volunteers. Makes sure all the tools have been returned at the end of day.

Photographer:
Captures the day's proceedings with eye-catching action shots and posed shots of smiling volunteers.

Large-tool Coordinators:
Delivers tools via truck to the participating teams. Drinking water should be included in the list of supplies, especially on a hot day.

Team Leaders:
Can be designated at the workday, but those with experience are recommended (particularly for tree plantings). These individuals guide their respective teams in proper practices, whether it's clearing debris, painting, or erecting a fence. Team assistants provide support by keeping track of the team's tools and ensuring they're returned.

Team leaders and assistants should also be enthusiastic and energetic. A team will be far more productive if morale is high and everyone is having fun. As always, take the time to appreciate and acknowledge the commitment of the volunteers.

With so many things to be done in a day, it's important to delegate and make sure each person fully understands what's expected. When everyone plays a part, it's amazing what can be accomplished.

Document Your Work

Make sure to designate a photographer for every workday and park event. Get pictures of people as well as the park. Pictures can be kept in a photo album or used in displays and flyers. Remember to take pictures before any large improvement projects.

After completion, take photos again—preferably from the same vantage point—to show the finished work. These pictures will make compelling before-and-after sets that document your progress in the park.

Chapter 5: Park Usage - Uniting your Community

Programming and Activities

Programming is a sure-fire way to involve the local community in the park. While not everyone in the neighborhood may volunteer to pull weeds or rake leaves, few can say no to a festival, farmers market, or concert.

Be sure to check in with the city and obtain any necessary permits, as well as check available dates. It's best to avoid conflicting interests with other users of the park outside of your group. Also, your city agency is a valuable partner that may have funds, personnel, or other resources to offer for the event.

For a first outing, select an event that requires only moderate coordination and expense. Something like an in-park yard sale or a potluck picnic is ideal because the attendees bring their own supplies. Once you have a sense of what is required to host an activity (including setup and cleanup), then plan to tackle more ambitious undertakings.

When planning an event, try to appeal to a variety of ages and interests. Spread the word about your event in the same way you would for a workday. Use the media (both online and print) to your advantage and hang banners and signs about town.

Have fun at the event, but be mindful of the park's immediate neighbors. Noise, trash, and excessive traffic could create resentment among those who would ideally be the park's top advocates.

Another thing to bear in mind is that it's possible to overbook your park. Every weekend doesn't have to be a huge celebration; sometimes it's best for the park just to be a park. Constant scheduling could easily wear down the park's resources and counteract all the cleaning and planting your group has performed.

Still, programming brings tremendous life and joy to a park. For a season-by-season list of engaging activities, see page 84.

Park events can vary widely in scope, from concerts to neighborhood parties to art shows, as seen here.

A Philadelphia Green Story
Summer in the Neighborhood

In well-populated areas there may be several parks in close proximity. Rather than viewing the parks as competing entities, unite them to pool resources and attract new group members.

In Philadelphia, many parks offer evening concerts; farmers markets; and a host of fun, family-friendly activities. Those who lived in the immediate vicinity of a park would flock to the events, but park leaders found it difficult to attract a wider audience.

In response to this dilemma, the Pennsylvania Horticultural Society's Philadelphia Green program worked with city government and friends-of-the-park groups to create a compilation of park events citywide. Called the "Summer in the Neighborhood" series, the promotion reached people through newspaper ads, website postings, and postcard-sized brochures that were placed in grocery store checkouts, libraries, train stations, and other high-volume places.

The impact was immediate. The first summer, people not only attended their local park event, but also branched out and experienced parks in other communities. Due to its success, "Summer in the Neighborhood" has returned every year since.

When it comes to hosting events, Gorgas Park, in the Roxborough neighborhood, has been one of the busiest. In addition to featuring several concerts each summer, Gorgas Park also offers movie nights, a harvest festival, and an annual community day. All this activity is made possible by a tireless friends group that understands the importance of exposure. In the weeks before an event, the group places advertisements in the local paper. As a result, the park celebrations are always well-attended.

Suggested Activities

SPRING
- Easter-egg hunt
- Mother's Day picnic
- Jazz concerts
- After-school programs
- Earth Day and
  Arbor Day festivities

AUTUMN
- Halloween parade
- Concerts (into early fall)
- Raking competitions
- Harvest fests

SUMMER
- Movie nights
- Barbeques
- Concerts
- Flea markets
- Fourth of July party
- Summer camps
- Chili cook-off

WINTER
- Holiday decorating; tree lighting
- Holiday caroling and hot cocoa
- Solstice celebration
- Snowman-making competition
- Wreath making

A Park for All

Involving the community in reclaiming your park will help ensure it meets residents' needs and reflects the neighborhood's character. This approach creates a sense of ownership among community members and may also help attract more support.

Think about who uses your park, and take into account the population of the neighborhood, including its ethnic makeup. For example, in South Philadelphia, an area with strong Italian roots, neighbors living around tiny Bardascino Park created a bocce court there. The court is heavily used and has become a neighborhood anchor, hosting regular games and even tournaments that bring everyone together. Another example can be found in eastern North Philadelphia, where Las Parcelas park and community garden serves as a gathering place where the community's predominantly Puerto Rican residents learn about and celebrate their rich cultural heritage.

Kids playing a game of bocce at Bardascino Park

Parks are a great place for youth and adults to interact and learn from each other.

In densely populated city neighborhoods, meeting the sometimes competing needs of park users can be a delicate balance. On the following pages, you will find ways to engage three groups of frequent park users: children, senior citizens, and dog owners. When planning workdays, events, or landscape improvements, bear these groups in mind.

Polish festival at Campbell Square Park

Children and Teens

With any parks projects you undertake, you'll want to consider how to involve all ages of children. Kids can undo a lot of tender loving care very quickly if they don't have a personal connection to your greening effort. But once you tap into kid energy, you will find that young park stewards feel very strongly about improving their communities. In addition, you can take advantage of their unlimited stamina and limber backs. In short, put them to work! Make sure to make it fun and give them plenty of positive reinforcement.

Schools

Park groups that are interested in working with schools will find many opportunities to interact with budding environmentalists. In addition, many teachers search for activities to satisfy district requirements mandating that students complete a "community-based service learning" project. An ideal service-learning experience combines academic content with hands-on activity, and many tasks relating to park care fit the bill. Some suggestions for service-learning projects include involving older students in a neighborhood park inventory project, or having students help research, plan, and implement park cleanups or activities.

After-school Programs

Contact your neighborhood schools about enriching their after-school program with some of these same activities. Establishing a youth park group during this period has the advantage of not competing with a teacher's instructional time during the day. Consider enlisting student help to pick up litter at both their schoolyard and the park, for example. Take advantage of the resources of organizations that already have extensive experience working with youth, such as Boy Scouts, Girl Scouts, and the 4-H Club.

Planning a Park Event for Youth

Develop partnerships with schools and other neighborhood institutions. Work together to plan and implement school programs. Consider piggybacking the event with a larger project or something happening in the neighborhood. This is a great time to kick off a new garden or planting, commemorate a community leader, or honor a neighbor.

Decide how many people to invite and where to have the program.

Involve different schools from the surrounding area. When offering the program to a school for the first time, bring written information such as a poster advertising the event or news articles about the park group.

Plan educational, entertaining, and interactive activities for the students. Consider the attention span of young children and plan activities that last just 15 to 20 minutes. Encourage students to create posters and banners, or perform songs and skits.

Invite local leaders and the press to attend the event. The more groups you have involved, the more newsworthy the event becomes. Make sure there are visually pleasing attractions for television and photo shoots. Include the following people on your invitation list: the mayor, school principal, city council members, and civic leaders.

A selection of youth-related educational activities:

- **Recycling games**
- **Arts and crafts**
- **Seed planting**
- **Storytelling**
- **Planting trees, shrubs, and flowers**
- **Tree mulching**

Senior Citizens

Seniors are often eager and appreciative park-goers, so what can you do to make your park more senior-friendly? Many suggestions can be found in a recent study conducted by Susan Rodiek, professor at Texas A&M University and associate director of the school's Center for Health Systems & Design.

According to her research, plenty of comfortable seating is top priority. Benches, chairs, and such should be found throughout the park so seniors don't have to travel long distances, regardless of their starting point. Place the seating in shady areas so the sun isn't overbearing.

On the other hand, if there is a particular place that seniors favor in your park, take that into account. For example, In Norris Square Park in North Philadelphia, several benches were placed on the east side of the park, where they offered access to seniors who lived in an assisted living facility across the street.

Consider installing stationary games near these seating areas. Philadelphia's East Park commissioned six concrete tables with built-in chess/checker boards. Some companies offer inlaid backgammon boards as well.

Rodiek's study also reveals that walking is a primary source of exercise for many seniors, so paved pathways are always well received. (Make sure they are in good condition with no hazards.) Interestingly, seniors prefer paths that make a loop as opposed to those with dead ends, as they provide a sense of accomplishment.

Another point Rodiek enforces is that older people do not want "to feel cut off from life." Include them in park activities from workdays to events. Even if they aren't up for heavy lifting, they are perfectly able to sign in volunteers, work a ticket booth, pass out tools, or perform any number of duties.

Dogs and their Owners

Dogs, like people, love to spend time in the park. But in order to make the park a pleasant place for everyone, pet owners should be gracious guests. Here are some suggestions:

Make rules and stick to them. Most of the rules regarding dogs seem obvious: dogs should remain on leashes, and owners must clean up after their animals, etc. But in order to erase uncertainty, post your park's rules in highly visible places. (The same holds true to all park rules, not exclusively those dealing with pets.)

Simplify the situation. If you want to keep your park free of dog droppings, make it easy for the owners by installing doggie stations (metal posts that dispense plastic bags for easy waste removal). Also have trash cans nearby.

Consider a dog run. If your park is a large tract of land, consider designating a certain plot specifically for the pooches. A fenced-in area with a water source allows dogs to be off leash for exercising and socializing. Remind pet owners, however, that they are responsible for their pet's behavior. Make sure there are bags available with a notice that owners must pick up waste.

Dog runs require a lot of maintenance. For instance, grass can't survive a dog pen, so the area may need a layer of woodchips. And those woodchips will need to be replenished regularly. Before establishing a dog run, be sure there's a strong enough interest among the community to sustain it.

Find financial backing. Because a dog run can be expensive to establish and operate, perhaps your park group should allow the dog run to have a semi-independent board or a separate committee with a distinct operating budget. (After all, those without dogs may resent the park's funds being funneled toward the dog run.)

Be prepared to apply for grants, host fundraisers, lobby local politicians, and explore other means of generating funding for the dog run. Understand the initial costs of setup and the additional annual costs of maintenance. With a well-planned, compelling proposal, you'll have no trouble rallying support among animal lovers.

Have fun! Pet lovers tend to be caring, compassionate people. If you'd like them to be advocates of the park, indulge them with canine-centric activities. Puppy parades are bound to be popular.

For more on establishing dog runs, see the Resources section.

Bringing Dogs to the Park

Prospect Park is a 585-acre oasis in Brooklyn, New York, that welcomes eight million visitors each year. To make the park enjoyable for those with and without dogs, the Prospect Park Alliance has established firm-but-fair leashing guidelines.

Each day, dogs are allowed to be off-leash from 5 am to 9 am and from 9 pm to 1 am at three designated locations. Dogs are even allowed to go swimming at the Long Meadow Dog Beach. Because the park has made such efforts to accommodate dog owners, they ask that dogs remain leashed at all other times and locations. There is a $100 fine for an unleashed dog.

This arrangement allows everyone to have a pleasant park experience. While Prospect Park has far more land than the average neighborhood park, the lesson to be learned is the importance of compromise. Dog owners and those without pets can happily coexist in the park so long as there are rules in place that respect and reflect the needs of all park users.

Chapter 6: Conclusion

Conclusion : Great Parks Make Great Neighborhoods

On a recent summer night in South Philadelphia, city dwellers relaxed on blankets and beach chairs in Mario Lanza Park, munching popcorn as *The Black Stallion* flickered on an outdoor movie screen. Several blocks away, in Jefferson Square Park, people swayed to the sounds of jazz and enjoyed a refreshing evening breeze.

Scenes like these were once unthinkable in Philadelphia, where for decades neighborhood parks were awash in crime, trash, and despair. But thanks to the hard work and commitment of thousands of volunteers and supporters, such gatherings are now commonplace all across the city.

Once places that were abandoned and actively avoided, today many of Philadelphia's neighborhood parks draw thousands of residents.

The partnerships that are transforming Philadelphia's parks have never been stronger. In the past 15 years, government has found ways to increase its investment, while private funders, the business community, and residents have stepped forward with assistance. Though challenges remain, there is a renewed sense of pride, purpose, and place.

Park groups are deeply invested in the progress of their parks and are ready, willing, and able to stand up and speak out for these cherished open spaces.

A recent study of the value of Philadelphia's parks and recreation system by the Trust for Public Land shows that a relatively small investment in parks reaps a huge return for the city. Author Peter Harnik writes, "The park system of Philadelphia thus provided the city with revenue of $23.3 million, municipal savings of $15.1 million, resident savings of $1.1 billion, and a collective increase of resident wealth of $729.1 million in 2007."

Comparable rewards surely accrue to cities everywhere. Harnik notes, "To attract and retain residents and businesses in the twenty-first century, cities have no choice but to provide residents with the best possible quality of life. Parks provide hundreds of millions of dollars worth of help."

So, as you go about the vital work of reclaiming your park, part of your job will include convincing others to support the parks you love. And the next time you hear, "We can't afford to spend money on parks," just reply, "We can't afford not to."

Although being part of a park group is a sizeable commitment, it helps to remember the reasons why you initially took on this challenge. When people come together to reclaim a park, they are essentially reclaiming their neighborhood. Well-maintained, active parks are found in strong communities with much to offer, from safe streets to a stable real estate market to a better quality of life. These strong communities make stronger cities.

As stated earlier, the benefits of attractive parks are many:

- **Parks provide natural beauty and become neighborhood gathering places and centers of community life.**
- **Parks offer play spaces for children and promote physical activity and better health for all.**
- **Parks improve the local environment by absorbing stormwater, improving air quality, reducing the "heat island" effect, and offering habitat for wildlife.**
- **Parks are "democratizing" spaces, open to all free of charge.**
- **Parks provide significant economic benefits to cities.**

What We've Learned

At this point you may be advancing your idea of a better park from a dream to a reality. In this manual, we have discussed what it takes to get there. Great parks need vision, leadership, planning, resources, partnerships, and stewardship.

In many cities, the old model of park management—relying on municipal government alone—is no longer feasible. By embracing a new model in which people work together to create thriving parks, cities will reap tremendous social benefits. People come together from a wide range of perspectives, including citizens, government, business, foundations, and nonprofits. Organizations working in partnership discover new possibilities.

In the process of transforming their parks, residents transform themselves into committed stewards of their neighborhoods. Very often, the process of reclaiming a park becomes a springboard for other improvements. Neighbors meet each other and discover common interests. Individuals discover previously untapped leadership skills and talents.

Successful park groups work together to create a shared vision. To do that, they must listen to all the voices in the neighborhood. They must work with their city government to find new ways of getting things done. They must dream up creative ways of raising money, raising awareness, and having fun. Along the way, they learn how to plant a tree, how to prune a shrub, and which flowers attract butterflies.

In short, parks are literally the "common ground" that brings people together to build strong, vibrant communities. PHS looks forward to being a resource for you as you carry out this extraordinary work!

Resources

ADVOCACY

Organizations and websites

City Parks Alliance *www.cityparksalliance.org*
City Parks Alliance is a national organization that
advocates for urban parks. It offers conferences,
publications, case studies, and trainings.

EBSCO GreenFILE *www.greeninfoonline.com*
This freely accessible database provides citations and
abstracts for approximately 295,000 articles on the
relationship between humans and the environment. The
full text of close to 5,000 articles is available.

National Recreation and Parks Association
www.nrpa.org
The NRPA is a national association of park and
recreation professionals that produces many resources and
publications relevant to parks.

Philadelphia Parks Alliance *www.philaparks.org*
The leading parks advocacy group in Philadelphia. See
Philadelphia Resources.

Project for Public Spaces *www.pps.org*
The New York-based Project for Public Spaces has a great
deal of online resources about parks, including case-
making, programming, and planning.

The Trust for Public Land *www.tpl.org*
TPL is home of the Center for City Park Excellence,
which offers data on comparative park systems, the
importance of parks, and the needs and opportunities for
parks. It also has information about the benefits of parks,
connections to health, and much more.

University of Washington, College of Forest Resources
www.cfr.washington.edu/research.envmind/
Research on the human benefits of urban greening. Offers
resources, printable studies, fact sheets, and helpful links.

Publications

Compton, John L. *The Impact of Parks and Open Space
on Property Values and the Property Tax Base.* National
Recreation and Park Association, 2000.

----. *Parks and Economic Development.* American
Planning Association, 2001.

Garvin, Alexander. *Parks, Recreation, and Open Space:
A Twenty-First Century Agenda.* American Planning
Association, 2000.

Garvin, Alexander and Gayle Berens. *Urban Parks and
Open Space.* Urban Land Institute, 1997.

Ginsburg, Kenneth R. et al. "*The Importance of
Play in Promoting Healthy Child Development and
Maintaining Strong Parent-Child Bonds.*" The American
Academy of Pediatrics. 2006.

Godbey, Geoffrey. *The Benefits of Local Recreation and
Park Services: A Nationwide Study of the Perceptions
of the American Public.* National Recreation and Park
Association, 1992.

Harnik, Peter. *The Excellent City Park System: What
Makes it Great and How to Get There.* The Trust for
Public Land, 2003.

----. "*How Much Value Does the City of Philadelphia
Receive from its Park and Recreation System?*"
The Trust for Public Land, 2008.

----. "*Inside City Parks.*" Urban Land Institute, The
Trust for Public Land, 2000.

Lewis, Megan. "*How cities use parks for ... Economic
Development.*" American Planning Association, City
Parks Forum briefing paper. 2002. Available at
www.planning.org/cpf.

Louv, Richard. *Last Child in the Woods: Saving our Children from Nature-Deficit Disorder.* Algonquin Books of Chapel Hill, 2005.

Low, Setha M. *Rethinking Urban Parks: Public Space & Cultural Diversity.* University of Texas Press, 2005.

Pennsylvania Horticultural Society. "Parks Revitalization: Celebrating 15 Years of Transformation." *Strategy for a Green City.* Spring, 2008.

----. "Greening: A Wise Investment." *Strategy for a Green City.* Fall, 2006.

Sherer, Paul M. *"The Benefits of Parks: Why America Needs More City Parks and Open Space."* The Trust for Public Land, 2006 (originally published in 2003).

COMMUNITY ENGAGEMENT, ORGANIZATION BUILDING, AND PARTNERSHIP

Organizations and websites

Neighborhood Link *www.neighborhoodlink.com*
Neighborhood Link is an Internet-based network that enables metropolitan-area neighborhood associations to create free, interactive websites.

Partnership for Parks *www.partnershipforparks.org*
Partnership for Parks is a joint program of the City Parks Foundation and the City of New York Parks and Recreation office. Its technical assistance program is geared for New Yorkers, but its website contains helpful information, downloadable tip sheets, and links.

Publications

Barker, Larry Lee. *Groups in Process: An Introduction to Small Group Communication.* Allyn and Bacon, 1995.

Chrislip, David D. *The Collaborative Leadership Fieldbook.* Jossey-Bass, 2002.

Grogan, Paul S. *Comeback Cities: A Blueprint for Urban Neighborhood Revival.* Westview Press, 2000.

Kretzmann, John P. and John L. McKnight. *Building Communities from the Inside Out: A Path Toward Finding and Mobilizing a Community's Assets.* The Asset-Based Community Development Institute, Northwestern University, 1993 (Distributor: ACTA Publications, Chicago, IL).

----. *Rediscovering Community Through Parks.* Lila Wallace-Reader's Digest Urban Parks Institute, 1997.

Myerson, Deborah L. *Parks, People and Places: Making Parks Accessible to the Community.* ULI–Urban Land Institute, 2006.

Pennsylvania Horticultural Society. "Partnerships: Collaboration + Empowerment = Success." *Strategy for a Green City.* Summer, 2007.

Rodiek, S. & Benyamin Schwarz. *The Role of the Outdoors in Residential Environments for Aging.* Haworth Press, 2006.

Urban Land Institute. *ULI Community Catalyst Report Number 1: Involving the Community in Neighborhood Planning.* ULI–Urban Land Institute, 2005.

Walker, Chris. *Partnerships for Parks: Lessons from the Lila Wallace-Reader's Digest Urban Parks Program.* Lila Wallace-Reader's Digest Urban Parks Institute, 1999.

DOG RUNS

Organizations and websites

Fido *www.fidobrooklyn.com*
A project of the dog owners of Prospect Park in Brooklyn, New York City, Fido is one of the leading dog advocacy groups with many resources on its website.

Urban Hound *http://ny.urbanhound.com/houndPlay /startingADogRun.asp*

American Kennel Club
Online article, "Establishing a Dog Park in Your Community"
www.akc.org/canine_legislation/dogpark.cfm

FUNDRAISING

Organizations and websites

The Foundation Center *http://foundationcenter.org*
The Foundation Center is a national organization that maintains a comprehensive database of foundations all over the country. It also offers books, courses, and other training resources for fundraising.

Publications

Klein, Kim. *Fundraising for Social Change*, 5th edition, Chardon Press series, 2007.

HORTICULTURE & LANDSCAPE MANAGEMENT

Organizations and websites

American Horticultural Society *www.ahs.org*

Compost
Visit *www.howtocompost.org*, consult your local library for books on composting, or contact your State Extension service for workshops and educational materials on compost.

Garden Web *www.gardenweb.com*

Hardiness Zones
The website of the United National Arboretum has a clickable zonal map indicating temperature ranges down to individual counties (*www.usna.usda.gov/Hardzone/ ushzmap.html*).

National Gardening Association *www.garden.org*

Pennsylvania Horticultural Society
www.pennsylvaniahorticulturalsociety.org
A membership organization founded in 1827, PHS produces the renowned Philadelphia Flower Show. PHS's Philadelphia Green is the nation's most comprehensive urban greening program (*www.philadelphiagreen.org*). PHS offers gardening workshops, the McLean Library, *Green Scene* magazine, publications and manuals on urban greening, Ask a Gardener information service (*askagardener@pennhort.org*), and more. PHS's McLean Library compiles a list of horticultural speakers available for presentations and workshops (*mcleanlibrary@pennhort.org*).

University of Minnesota Libraries, Plant Information Online
https://plantinfo.umn.edu/arboretum/default.asp
Sources for more than 10,000 plants, citations for garden literature, links to selected websites, regional information about more than 12,000 plants, and information on North American seed and nursery firms.

University of Delaware Center for Public Horticulture
www.publichorticulture.udel.edu
The University of Delaware's Center for Public Horticulture seeks to become a clearinghouse for education and research in public horticulture.

Landscape Architecture Image Resource
www.lair.umd.edu
The Landscape Architecture Image Resource (LAIR) is a collaborative effort by the landscape architecture faculties of several universities. You don't need to be a landscape architecture student, teacher, or practitioner to enjoy and learn from this site.

Site/Lines
www.foundationforlandscapestudies.org/index. php?p=sitelines
Site/Lines is a journal of the Foundation for Landscape Studies that "occupies a niche in the middle ground between the scholarly journal and the garden magazine." Its full text is available free at the foundation's website.

Publications

Cranz, Galen. *The Politics of Park Design: A History of Urban Parks in America.* MIT Press, 1982.

Damrosch, Barbara. *The Garden Primer* (second edition). Workman Publishing Company, Inc., 2008.

Forsyth, Ann. *Designing Small Parks: A Manual Addressing Social and Ecological Concerns.* J. Wiley, 2005.

Faga, Barbara. *Designing Public Consensus: The Civic Theater of Community Participation for Architects, Landscape Architects, Planners, and Urban Designers.* John Wiley & Sons, Inc., 2006.

Pepper, Jane G. *Jane Pepper's Garden: Getting the Most Pleasure and Growing Results From Your Garden Every Month of the Year.* Camino Books, 1997.

MEETING MANAGEMENT

Mind Tools
www.mindtools.com/CommSkll/RunningMeetings.htm

"Running a Meeting"
Printable guide from the Massachusetts Institute of Technology website:
http://web.mit.edu/2.009/www/resources /mediaAndArticles/3_MeetingPrimer.pdf

PLAYGROUNDS

Organizations and websites

KaBOOM! *www.kaboom.org*
KaBOOM! is a national nonprofit organization that provides planning tools for organizing community play-space building projects. It offers online training as well as a limited number of challenge grants.

TREES

Organizations and websites

American Forests
www.americanforests.org

International Society of Arboriculture
www.isa-arbor.com

The National Arbor Day Foundation
www.arborday.org

Pennsylvania Horticultural Society
www.pennsylvaniahorticulturalsociety.org
Tree Tenders training program, videos on tree planting

TreeLink *www.treelink.org*
TreeLink is an organization that seeks to raise awareness and support for healthy urban forests.

Trees Are Good *www.treesaregood.com*
Trees Are Good is an educational website that offers practical information on tree care, as well as information on the benefits and value of trees.

Publications

"Planting and After Care of Community Trees." Penn State College of Agricultural Sciences, Agricultural Research and Cooperative Extension, downloadable brochure on care of community trees
http://pubs.cas.psu.edu/freepubs/pdfs/uh143.pdf

WORKING WITH CHILDREN & YOUTH

Organizations and websites

American Horticulture Society
www.ahs.org/youth_gardening
Annual National Children & Youth Gardening Symposium

Children & Nature Network *www.cnaturenet.org*

Earth Force
www.earthforce.org/section/resources/activites
A national nonprofit, Earth Force's website offers many resources for youth activities in parks.

www.kidsgardening.com
Website with gardening ideas and resources for teachers and parents

Pennsylvania Association of Environmental Educators
www.paee.net

WORKING WITH VOLUNTEERS

Organizations and websites

Association for Volunteer Resource Management
www.AVRM.org
This is targeted to those who lead/manage/coordinate volunteers.

Idealist *www.idealist.org*
Idealist.org maintains an interactive website with resources and information for volunteers.

Points of Light *www.pointsoflight.org*
A national organization dedicated to volunteers and management of volunteer programs with lots of resources on its website.

Service Leader *www.serviceleader.org*
This website is geared toward volunteer management.

Publications

Vineyard, Sue. *Handling Problem Volunteers*. Heritage Arts Publishing, 1998.

PHILADELPHIA RESOURCES

Community Design Collaborative
www.cdesignc.org
1216 Arch Street, First Floor
Philadelphia, PA 19107
215-587-9290
The Community Design Collaborative is a volunteer organization that offers preliminary design assistance to nonprofits. The Collaborative meets with nonprofits at the beginning of a project, develops a scope of services to fit their needs, and recruits design professionals to provide the services pro bono.

Energize Inc. *www.energizeinc.com*
5450 Wissahickon Avenue
Philadelphia, PA 19144
215-438-8342
The website of Energize Inc. offers many resources on volunteer management, and its reference library is open by appointment.

Fairmount Park Commission*
www.fairmountpark.org
One Parkway, 10th Floor
1515 Arch Street
Philadelphia, PA 19102
215-683-0200

GreenPlan Philadelphia
www.greenplanphiladelphia.com
The city's first comprehensive open space plan

Philadelphia City Council
Find your local City Council representative at *www.phila.gov/citycouncil/*.

Philadelphia Department of Recreation*
www.phila.gov/recreation
1515 Arch Street, 10th Floor
Philadelphia, PA 19102
215-683-3600

Philadelphia Green Parks Revitalization Project
www.philadelphiagreen.org
The Pennsylvania Horticultural Society
100 N. 20th Street, 5th Floor
Philadelphia, PA 19103
215-988-8800, *parks@pennhort.org*

Philadelphia Parks Alliance
www.philaparks.org
P.O. Box 12677
Philadelphia, PA 19129
215-879-8159
The leading parks advocacy group in Philadelphia

*Please note: The Philadelphia Department of Recreation
and the Fairmount Park Commission have merged. Please
check *www.phila.gov* for updated contact information.

Index